MARKING THE MILES

A History of English Milestones

CAROL HAINES

First published in Great Britain in 2000 by Carol Haines

© Carol Haines, 2000

ISBN: 0-9538885-0-9

Printed by Crowes Complete Print, Norwich, Norfolk

Front cover: A625, Mam Tor (Derbys.)

Back cover: *Left*: Ullesthorpe (Leics.)
                    Right: Shooters Hill (London)

There is poetry in the commonplace, if only
we could keep our eyes open to see it.

The Button Box, Alison Uttley

For Alan, Neal and Mark

Contents

Marking the Miles

Southwark obelisk (see p.94) has now been moved back to St George's Circus where it forms the centre of a large traffic island. Since undertaking research for this book other milestones may, unfortunately, have been damaged or lost, but others have been found. For further details see: www.milestonesociety.co.uk

Acknowledgements

Boredom on long road journeys directed my attention and curiosity to milestones, and the difficulty of finding information on their history provided the impetus for this book. Because nothing has previously been written in detail on the subject, a great deal of research has been required. This has necessitated the help of so many people that it is impossible to name them all individually. Librarians and archivists all over England have been most patient and helpful and have unearthed invaluable information. Many other people have provided sightings, anecdotes, photographs, or beautifully detailed drawings. To all of them I offer my sincere thanks.

Those who deserve special mention are D. Hamilton for information on Suffolk; Robert Haynes for information on Wiltshire; Steve Lister for help with Lancashire, Cumbria and West Yorkshire; Alan Rosevear for details from Berkshire and Oxfordshire; and John Taylor for information from Lancashire. The following people have kindly allowed me to reproduce their photographs: Steve Lister (nos.20, 23, 33,), and Stuart Hands (no.6). All other photographs are my own.

I am grateful to Faber & Faber Ltd for permission to quote from *The Button Box* and *Country Things* by Alison Uttley.

Finally I must thank my husband Alan for his constant encouragement, for casting a critical eye over the manuscript and for the use of his computing skills, without which this book would not have been published.

Abbreviations

County boundaries have caused considerable problems. Since the advent of the county councils in 1888, and especially since the upheavals of 1974, there have been significant alterations in county boundaries which result in some milestones crossing the borders. To add to the confusion, some regional surveys of milestones were undertaken in the 1960s before the major boundary changes of 1974 and many milestones have now migrated to neighbouring counties, or to completely new ones. All these boundary changes were purely for administrative purposes, and although the ancient geographical counties have remained the same, modern maps do not indicate their margins. For the purposes of this book, the boundaries used are those found on Ordnance Survey maps, which follow administrative rather than geographical borders. Where a county has several divisions, such as North, South and West Yorkshire, or East and West Sussex, milestones have been placed simply in Yorkshire or Sussex, because a series may inconsiderately meander through modern dividing lines. Where London is indicated, the boundaries of Greater London have been used as denoted by the Ordnance Survey. Thus Bromley, for example, has been listed under London rather than Kent. The longer county names have been abbreviated in the text as follows:

Beds.	Bedfordshire
Berks.	Berkshire
Bucks.	Buckinghamshire
Cambs.	Cambridgeshire (including Huntingdonshire)
Derbys.	Derbyshire
Glos.	Gloucestershire
Hants	Hampshire
Her. & Worcs.	Hereford & Worcester

Herts.	Hertfordshire
Lancs.	Lancashire
Leics.	Leicestershire (including Rutland)
Lincs.	Lincolnshire
Northants	Northamptonshire
Northumb.	Northumberland
Notts.	Nottinghamshire
Oxon	Oxfordshire
Salop	Shropshire
Staffs.	Staffordshire
Warwicks.	Warwickshire
Wilts.	Wiltshire
Yorks.	Yorkshire

CHAPTER 1

Introduction

Some of the most neglected features of this country are the milestones dotted along our highways. They are easily overlooked as we speed past, and many are being damaged or destroyed during road alterations or maintenance. We are thus in danger of losing fascinating pieces of our history, although the word 'milestone' is still in very common use today to describe significant events from which to measure other achievements. While many milestones are still carefully tended by local authorities and are regularly painted and renovated, others are neglected and become hidden in vegetation, buried in roadside banks, damaged during verge cutting, or eroded by salt spray and general pollution.

Roman milestones are now mostly safe in museums, and while we may not want all our history on display in glass cases, it might be necessary to protect a few more eighteenth- and nineteenth-century examples in this way. Left where they stand, however, they will tell us much more about the history of roads and travel in this country, and every effort should be made to protect them since every one of them is unique.

Milestones always seem to have been taken for granted. Even travellers of the past who progressed at a much slower pace made little mention of them, although they would have been a very common sight from the mid-eighteenth century, and would have been of great importance in letting people know how much more of a tedious, uncomfortable journey they had to endure. The praise is left to foreign visitors such as Carl-Philip Moritz, a German pastor on a walking holiday in England in 1782, who wrote during his journey from London to Oxford:

1

'The English milestones are a great convenience for travellers; they have often seemed to relieve me of half the distance because I am always anxious to know how far I have come and if I am on the right road. The distance from London is always given on these milestones together with the distance to the next town.'

The Romans introduced milestones throughout their empire and remains of them have been found as far afield as France, Spain, North Africa, Israel and the Balkans as well as in Britain. Over four thousand have been found, the earliest dating from 252 BC.

Distance markers can be found in other countries today, with most motorways having small metal plates of varying colours. Other main roads often have a modern equivalent of a milestone. In Belgium, triangular posts of red and white plastic give the kilometres and the road number. Present-day French roads have kilometre posts of a standard pattern, the arched top being painted red on the Routes Nationales and yellow on the less important Routes Departmentales. Spain and Portugal have similar markers. Older kilometre stones can be found in Germany and Switzerland, but usually only denoting the distance and not the destination. At Wilderswill near Interlaken, Switzerland is a stone reading 'XII Stunden von BERN'. Maintaining an average walking pace with a few rest periods on the way, would indeed allow one to cover the fifty kilometres from Bern in twelve hours.

France is one of the few countries where some of the kilometre stones repay closer scrutiny. The only individual French road allowed a name rather than a number is 'La Voie Sacrée' from Bar-le-Duc to Verdun. It was named by General Pétain during World War I for the rôle it played in supplying the army fighting around Verdun. As the only available main route, it was in constant use day and night with a truck passing along it on average every fourteen seconds for most of 1916. Its marker stones are also unique, being rectangular pillars topped by a bronze helmet. They give a town name, although not a distance. In northern France the name 'La Voie de la Liberté' was given to a network of roads to commemorate the sacrifice of American troops in liberating the country following the D-Day landings of World War II. Along many roads, mainly in Normandy, can be found special kilometre posts showing a flaming torch and one of these is possibly the only milestone ever to have been featured on a postage stamp. Kilometre Zero is in front of the Mairie in Sainte-Mère-Eglise, the first town to be liberated on the night of 5-6 June 1944. The 'Voie de la Liberté' was the idea of the French liaison officer with the American army and Kilometre Zero was inaugurated on 16 September 1947.

Only in Britain, however, did the practice of erecting milestones resurface with such enthusiasm and eccentricity. The first were put on the Dover road in 1633 by the postal authorities. From the early eighteenth century landowners put them up to guide visitors to their estates or as status symbols, and they came into wider use with the advent of the turnpikes. Towns and parishes were also responsible for many milestones, while a few were paid for by public subscription. After their formation at the end of the nineteenth century, some of the county and rural district councils also erected these markers. From the early simple, square or 'tombstone' shapes, often using Roman numerals, designs changed to make them more readable to travellers. Some regions of England have styles unique to that area, possibly because local craftsmen copied the shapes of other objects they were familiar with making and because of the availability of materials to manufacture them.

Milestones were also introduced into some of the British colonies. Maidstone Museum has the forty-four mile stone from the Ipoh to Kuala Lumpur road, which was brought back from Malaysia in the 1950s by the Royal West Kent Regiment. The triangular-plan stone has a large piece missing from one side where it was hit by bullets during a skirmish with bandits. Stones can be found as far away as India and Australia, and in 1836 Charles Darwin remarked on the presence of milestones along the main cart-road across the bleak, remote island of Ascension.

Although milestones are to be found in all parts of the United Kingdom, this present study has been confined to

3

England because of the difficulty of gathering information from every county. It is impossible to say how many still remain in England. Where previous studies have been undertaken, Wiltshire was found to have over four hundred, Hampshire and Norfolk over three hundred, and Berkshire and Somerset also a considerable number. In general, counties in the centre of England have lost more of their milestones, especially the small wayside stones, which probably disappeared during the extensive road developments of the 1960s. Warwickshire appears to have very few left, while a survey in Nottinghamshire found about thirty-five and another in Bedfordshire recorded only two. The milestones that do remain in these central counties tend to be the larger, more unusual structures.

The mile itself may soon be obsolete as the metrication of Britain continues. This measure of distance has had a chequered history, and it is only since the mid-nineteenth century that the 1,760 yard mile has been adopted nationally. The increasing use of the statute mile was hastened by its use by the postal authorities, the turnpike trusts, and the publication of increasingly sophisticated maps until it became essential to standardise the measurement in 1824.

Milestones are generally classed as 'street furniture' along with such objects as direction signs, horse troughs, lamp posts and pillar boxes. Because of their links with the roads themselves, they come under the heading of industrial archaeology, and references to them can be found in many books on this subject, some of which are listed in the Bibliography.

These markers have been referred to generally as mile*stones*, but to be exact this term should really only be used for those made principally of stone. Those of cast iron are mile*posts*, and on Ordnance Survey maps they are marked as MS or MP accordingly. However, other materials such as concrete and wood have been used, along with combinations of all these materials, and a generalised term covering them all seems simpler. 'Mileage markers' might be a more accurate term, as painted wooden boards and inscribed stone slabs set in walls have also been included in this present study. Canals and railways also have milestones, but this book only deals with those associated with roads.

As many examples as possible have been given in an attempt to show the very wide diversity of milestones that can still be found beside English roads, from small, insignificant stones scarcely noticed in the grass, to imposing obelisks and monuments. Some had a dual purpose and, besides giving distances, also served as lamp standards, water pumps or memorials. When their primary function was over, milestones have found uses as building material, gateposts, and even garden ornaments. They have also become local landmarks and around the country there are many Milestone Lanes, Houses, Hotels and Farms. Wherever possible the milestones mentioned in the book have been checked, but it has not been possible to visit all of them whose location has been obtained from surveys, and some may have been damaged or, sadly, may have disappeared altogether during the period of research and writing.

Their appearance in literature mainly reflects a homely, dependable quality, and references to them can be found among the wealth of classic English writing that was produced during the great era of turnpikes and stage-coach travel.

A study of milestones can tell us much about local history. They can be used to trace the routes of the old turnpike roads, indicate which other roads were well used in the eighteenth and nineteenth centuries, and even show the interests and eccentricities of the gentry, and the building fashion of the time. Where archive evidence can be found, something can be learnt of the craftsmen who made them and the efficiency and state of finances of the turnpike trusts who commissioned many of them.

A few concerned individuals and some county industrial archaeology societies have catalogued the remaining milestones in their area, but a great many remain to be documented. The final chapter of this book gives some ideas of how to track them down and research their history, in the hope that more interest will be awakened before too many more milestones disappear.

For the last few decades some lone voices have been pressing for more research to be done on milestones before it is too late. It is just ignorance of them that puts them in danger, and if interest can be aroused at a local level, much can be done to save them. If background information can be given on an endangered milestone, its chances of survival will be much greater. This kind of survey can be done by an individual or a small group and will be of value also to local historians.

Although about four hundred milestones have been described in the following chapters, they represent only a small proportion of the thousands still to be found in England. It is hoped that this book, the first comprehensive account of the subject, will stimulate an interest in milestones and help to save those that remain.

CHAPTER 2

The English Road

To understand the history of milestones, it is necessary to know something about the history of roads in England, and their administration. As a great deal has already been written on this subject, only a brief outline is given here in order to illustrate when milestones were erected and by whom. Many books dealing with the development of roads in this country are listed in the Bibliography for those who wish to find out more about this fascinating subject.

Prehistory

Prehistoric man must have travelled across the country hunting wild animals for food, and later herding livestock in the search for fresh grazing. He also needed to find flint for tools and weapons, salt for preserving food, and clay for making pots. The safest and easiest routes were often along watersheds or ridges, and tracks were gradually created. The best known are the ridgeway paths along the chalk Downs of southern England, but finding historical evidence to prove when these tracks were in use is extremely difficult and has mainly relied on the presence of settlements, forts, or burial sites nearby. Archaeological remains of tracks and associated settlements in lowland areas have often not survived so well and we may therefore have a distorted picture of early routes. Many of these ancient tracks were later used and altered by the Romans, the turnpike trusts, the cattle drovers, and in modern times have become tarmac roads or long-distance footpaths. In areas of extensive low-lying land such as the Somerset Levels and the East Anglian Fens increasing archaeological evidence is showing that wooden causeways were made to allow passage across large tracts of marshy ground. A section of the 'Sweet Track', a six thousand year old plank and rail causeway excavated in the Somerset Levels, can be seen in the British Museum. As overseas trade developed, with the export of such minerals as tin and lead, tracks led to ports on the coast or on rivers.

In his book *The Old Straight Track* (1925), Alfred Watkins noted the alignments of such features as large boulders, tumuli, hills and moats, and concluded that ancient peoples had created these alignments of landmarks for guiding travellers and traders on the straightest routes across the country. This became his theory of 'ley lines', so called because many places and features along these alignments incorporated the element 'ley', 'lee', 'leigh' etc. in the name. He also suggested that the figure of the Long Man of Wilmington cut into the chalk of the Sussex Downs depicted an early surveyor with his surveying staff. There is no proof whatsoever that his idea is correct, and with so many such features in the British landscape it is not difficult to align some of them to fit his theory.

The Roman Period

The Romans knew that the best way to hold their far-flung empire together was with a good road system. On their arrival in Britain in AD 43, they took over many of the ancient trackways and improved them. They also set about building over eight thousand miles of roads, the most important of which were the military roads to enable their armies to move rapidly to outlying parts of their empire. After the capital was established in London, major trunk roads spread out from there to all parts of the occupied country. Rome depended a great deal on imports, and trade routes were also essential, especially to south coast ports such as Dover and Chichester. Many other minor local roads developed, such as the network of routes from iron mines in the Weald and lead mines in the Pennines, and roads to serve the needs of the new settlements. Initial road development would have been organised by the Roman military authorities, while later trunk roads were planned and financed by the provincial government in London. Local roads were paid for by the local tribal administration, and it was the responsibility of a landowner to maintain a road crossing his land.

The Romans were the first to use genuine milestones, and about 110, most of them with inscriptions, have been found in Britain. Their main purpose seems to have been to remind the population of the name of the reigning emperor, and they usually record details of his titles, lineage and achievements. The mileage follows almost as an afterthought, and is sometimes not recorded at all. A Roman milestone found near Leicester (Ratae) reads: 'The Emperor Caesar Trajan Hadrian Augustus, son of the deified Trajan, conqueror of Parthia, grandson of the deified Nerva, father of his country, in the fourth year of tribunician power, thrice consul. From Ratae, 2 miles' (1).[1] Other milestones just refer to the local authority (civitas) which built or repaired the road, such as a stone inscribed R.P.C.D. (Respublica Civitatis Dobunnorum) from Kenchester (Her. & Worcs.) (for further details see Chapter 4). Some milestones had the inscriptions recut as emperors changed. A few bear no carved inscription at all; they may originally have had painted lettering.

1 *Roman milestone (Leicester)*

In the Forum in Rome are the remains of the Golden Milestone (Miliarium Aureum), a marble pillar four feet in diameter which had gilded bronze plaques recording the mileages to principal cities of the Empire. It was erected by Augustus in 20 BC. Other cities probably also had a principal milestone to help travellers setting off on long

9

journeys. The Tongres Milestone, now in a museum in Brussels, gives distances to Cologne, Worms, Rheims and Amiens, while the Autun Milestone gives details of roads to Rome, the Rhine and the Saône, as well as of local routes. Autun in Burgundy was at one time the leading city of Roman Gaul. Another milestone found in Luxembourg lists the posting stations from Mainz to Trier. Evidence of a similar stone having stood in Cadiz comes from the Vicarello goblets, now kept in the

National Museum of the Thermae in Rome. The four silver goblets are pillar-shaped, and bear lists of the posting-stations between Cadiz and Rome. They may have been modelled on a milestone and sold as souvenirs to soldiers. Two enamelled cups have also been found listing the forts along part of Hadrian's Wall. The practice is continued today, with most capital cities having a central point from which the main national routes are measured, such as the fine stone in Budapest (**2**) (see also Chapter 3 for datum points).

2 *Kilometre zero (Budapest)*

It is thought that the Romans calculated mileages in Britain from the 'London Stone', the remnants of which are now in the wall of a Chinese Bank in Cannon Street. The first record of it is in the late twelfth century with a reference to Henry, son of Eylwin of Londenstane who later became Lord Mayor of London. However, it already seems to have acquired a tradition and veneration going back much further. Possibly because of its age and because it was almost in the centre of the city, it had become an important symbol of power and leadership. 'Enter Jack Cade and his followers. He strikes his staff on London-

10

stone' and declares that he is lord of the city. This extract from Shakespeare's introduction to *2 Henry VI* Act IV, Scene vii was taken from an earlier account by Holinshead. During rebuilding work after the Great Fire of London, Sir Christopher Wren saw foundations below the stone in Cannon Street and thought that it formed part of a much larger monument. London Stone continued to stand as a stump in the street until 1742, when it was considered too much of a traffic hazard. The top was removed and placed in the south wall of St Swithin's church in Cannon Street. The church was bombed during World War II, and when the site was cleared and redeveloped in the 1960s, it was stipulated that London Stone be preserved in the new building. Only the rounded top, made of limestone from Clipsham in the Chilterns, remains. Archaeologists have plotted the position of London Stone as being in the centre of what was probably the gateway to the Governor's Palace in Roman London, where they would have expected such a milestone to stand. More of it probably remains to be found.

From the Saxons to the Stuarts

Little is known about the road system after Roman rule ended in AD 410, but as neglected roads would soon have become overgrown, many Roman roads must have continued in use, perhaps not always as main routes, but with enough traffic to ensure that vegetation was kept at bay. The Saxons were mainly farmers who settled in valleys near water and established self-sufficient communities and the roads that evolved were principally droveways and green lanes for moving cattle. Other invaders at that time, such as the Vikings, were sea-going people, who would probably have felt more at home on rivers than on roads.

After the Norman conquest communities were centred around a castle or monastery, and with a more stable society and centralised administration travelling increased again. Pilgrim routes came into being when people began to visit religious centres with holy relics, and beside them arose wayside crosses, often paid for as a form of penance by wealthier pilgrims. There are at least sixty pilgrim roads in England, but the most famous, the Pilgrims' Way from Winchester to Canterbury, follows an even older prehistoric track. Religious institutions paid for the upkeep of roads linking their often vast estates, a practice which ended with the dissolution of the monasteries. In areas with a sparse, widely-scattered population, many miles had to be travelled to the parish church to take the dead for burial. In some places special tracks were used almost solely for this purpose, and corpse roads can still be traced in such regions as the Lake District, Devon and Cornwall. Not all wayside crosses were of religious significance. On Dartmoor there are still about one hundred stone crosses to be found which were erected in the Middle Ages to guide travellers across the moor to market towns.[2]

Fairs were established and important roads linking major market towns were given royal protection in case the monarch wished to use them, and to safeguard other travellers, and this is the origin of the expression 'The King's Highway' - a perpetual right of passage for the sovereign and his subjects over another's land. English kings insisted on road maintenance carried out by local inhabitants to speed the movement of armies or central authorities, and for the government, which travelled with the monarch, and in medieval times monarchs spent much time on the move.

From 1555 parishes were made liable for the upkeep of roads passing through them and parishioners were obliged to spend four days a year working on the roads. In 1563 this was increased to six days. An unpaid Surveyor of Highways was appointed to oversee the work. River and coastal shipping was also important, especially for large loads, which could be transported more quickly, more cheaply and by fewer people. There were disadvantages however, as goods still had to be brought to the ports by packhorse or wagon, and many towns were situated some distance from navigable waterways. Road traffic increased as mills were built on rivers and as wars made journeys by sea more hazardous. On 25 September 1695, John Evelyn commented in his diary that national shipping losses had been immense because of the war between England and France. His friend Captain Gifford had just lost £70,000 when his ship was taken by French men-of-war near the English coast. The weather was also a major drawback as river craft could be delayed by floods, low water in times of drought, or ice in winter, and goods could be damaged by storms. Daniel Defoe tells how two hundred empty colliers going to fetch coal from Newcastle to London were caught by a storm while sailing across The Wash in 1692. One hundred and forty of them were wrecked. The creation of canals began in the 1760s, first for transporting coal in the Manchester area. Passenger services were developed, and travel was far more comfortable than by road. However, canals were much more limited in their extent, took far longer to build, and because of the work involved were only developed as and when money was available. Differences in lock and bridge sizes meant that goods often had to be trans-shipped, and in some areas containers were made that could be loaded, with their cargo inside, on to barges or carts. Innovations in the design of carriages meant that road travel gradually became more comfortable, and even in the early seventeenth century Thames watermen were beginning to lose business to Hackney coaches.

With all the limitations with water transport, roads began to resume their importance. In upland areas goods were principally transported by strings of packhorses while heavy, cumbersome wagons were used in lowland England. Travellers usually rode on horseback. Parishes with well-used roads running through them could no longer cope with the repairs, especially where the soil was heavy clay that soon became waterlogged. Celia Fiennes wrote much about bad roads in her travel journals. In 1697 she says: 'From thence [Woburn] we came to Dunstable over a sad road called Hockley in the Hole [Hockliffe] as full of deep slows [sloughs] in the winter it must be impassable.' In his *Tour Through the Whole Island of Great Britain*, published 1724-26, Daniel Defoe noted the appalling state of the roads on clay soil and 'the great number of horses every year kill'd by the excess of labour in those heavy ways'.

In Sussex, he was amazed by the sight of 'an ancient lady ... drawn to church in her coach with six oxen; nor was it done in frolic or humour, but meer necessity, the way being so stiff and deep, that no horses could go in it.' In the eighteenth century it could take three years to haul timber from mid-Sussex to Chatham because the roads were impassable in winter. Dr John Burton, who travelled through Sussex in 1751, thought that the people there had long legs because the bones had been lengthened by their constantly pulling their feet out of the mud! In 1763 Horace Walpole noted that the soil of Northamptonshire was like a 'clay pudding stuck full of villages'. Writing in 1767, Arthur Young considered the road from Billericay to Tilbury (Essex) a disgrace to the kingdom. Chalk wagons using it often needed twenty to thirty horses to drag each one out of the deep ruts. London businessmen took lodgings for their families in Epsom for the summer and commuted to the City daily on horseback. In winter the town was almost deserted because the roads were impassable. Wagons had made their appearance in the early seventeenth century, drawn by up to ten horses. These did great damage to the highways, and over the next two centuries great efforts were made to prevent traffic damaging the roads by restricting the numbers of draught animals, reducing the weight of loads and increasing the width of wheel treads. No thought was given to adapting road construction to suit the traffic.

There are many instances of private benefactors giving money for the upkeep of roads and bridges. This was often called 'Causey' (causeway) Money. William Wheler left 40d. ($16^1/_2$p) in his will when he died in 1416 'for the repair of bad and foul ways' in North Weald Bassett (Essex). When a Wiltshire pedlar by the name of Maud Heath died in 1474, she left an income of '£8 a year forever', derived from land and property, to be used for the repair of the road and causeway from Wick Hill to Chippenham where she had regularly taken her wares to sell. This causeway can still be seen. In 1592, the founder of Harrow School, John Lyon, made money available for the upkeep of the road from Harrow to London. In the late sixteenth century, the Master of Trinity Hall, Cambridge left money in his will to be used for mending the road from Cambridge to Barkway, no doubt to speed the journeys of fellow dons to and from London. In 1725, money from the trust was used to erect milestones on the road (see Chapter 4). Near Attleborough in Norfolk is a pillar called the Dial Stone with the following inscription: 'This Pillar was erected by the order of the Sessions of the Peace for Norfolk as a Gratefull Remembrance of the Charity of Sr. Edwin Rich Knt., who freely gave ye sume of Two Hundred pounds towards ye repaire of ye Highway between Wymondham and Attleborough A.D. 1675'. Celia Fiennes passed that way in 1698 and recorded that the country was 'low and moorish and the road on the Causey was in many

3 *Canterbury (Kent)*

places full of holes, tho' its secured by a barr at which passengers pay a penny a horse in order to the mending of the way, for all about it not to be rode on unless its a very dry summer.' This stretch of road had become the third turnpike road to be created in England in 1695. A stone in Canterbury High Street (Kent) (3) informs passers-by that the nearby bridge was widened nineteen feet in 1769 for the greater safety and convenience of passengers. The money to pay for the work was raised by voluntary contributions from the city and its neighbourhood. Although the tollbridge at Whitney-on-Wye (Her. & Worcs.) required an Act of Parliament to sanction its construction in 1780, five gentlemen living in the neighbourhood undertook to pay for the building and maintenance of the bridge, which was to replace the ferry across the river Wye. They were authorised to build a tollhouse and to collect payment from travellers to defray the expenses incurred. This tollbridge is still in operation today.

The road between Dover and London had been one of the busiest highways since Roman times. Dover was the principal port of entry for travellers to and from the Continent as it was the shortest sea crossing. In 1633, 'the postmaster's deputies and the hackneymen 'of Dover and Canterbury admeasured the highway between those two places, and set up posts at every mile's end, and expressed the same to be 15 miles and a quarter'.[3] This is the first record of mile markers in Britain since Roman times. They were probably rough posts of stone or wood, possibly with the mileage painted on them, and their main purpose was to determine the cost of hiring horses for the journey (see also Chapter 3).

The enclosure of arable land had probably started in medieval times when it was found that a block of land belonging to one farmer was easier to cultivate than a large open field under communal ownership. Field strips were exchanged or bought and the new blocks of land surrounded by a hedge or ditch to mark the boundary. From the mid eighteenth century the pace of enclosure quickened dramatically, especially in the Midlands, and brought with it the enclosure roads running along field boundaries and often straight or having the occasional right-angled bend. These roads are generally of great width (at least thirteen metres) to allow for traffic to make detours round stretches made impassable by winter rain.

Milestones began to appear again in the eighteenth century. Some were set up by landowners to help guide visitors to their country estates. In 1754 the landlord of the White Hart Inn at Bodmin paid for twenty-two milestones across Bodmin Moor to guide travellers to his hostelry, and it is probable that many other innkeepers placed some kind of mileage marker near their premises for the benefit of customers. The Highgate Hotel in Kendal (Cumbria), which dates from 1769, has a pair of cylindrical milestones either side of the entrance, one showing

135 miles to Edinburgh, the other 258 miles to London, presumably for the benefit of long-distance coach travellers. Other milestones were paid for by public subscription. The following paragraph appeared in the *Ipswich Journal* on 7 September 1751: 'A Subscription has been some time on foot for continuing the Mile Stones in the London Road, from Dedham in Essex to Yarmouth Bridge: the Expence of which is computed at £97 10s. [£97.50]. A list of some of the present Subscribers may be seen at Potter's and Robin's Coffee-Houses in this Town: and a further Account of the Design, and the Success it meets with, will be shortly published in this Paper.' A report two months later suggests that the money was raised and the stones put in place. In Norfolk eighteen subscribers collected £9 7s. 0d. (£9.35) to pay for milestones on the Norwich to East Dereham road in 1755. A milestone near Tonwell (Herts.), whose mileage to London is now hardly readable, has a clear inscription on the back reading 'Repaired by a Voluntary Subscription From the Inhabitants of Ware 1751'. It is not clear whether this refers to the milestone or to the Watton to Ware road, which was not turnpiked until 1757.

Since the end of the Roman occupation, new roads had slowly evolved rather than been created. The next great construction period came with the introduction of the turnpike system in the late seventeenth century.

Turnpikes

For some time the idea of making travellers pay for road repairs had been discussed, but it was not until 1663 that the first toll road was set up between Wadesmill and Stilton on the Great North Road, administered by local Justices of the Peace. The first turnpike trust was started in 1706 between Fornhill and Stony Stratford. By an Act of Parliament, a group of trustees was authorised to erect tollgates, collect tolls, appoint surveyors and undertake road repairs. Many of the trustees were local businessmen or landowners with a vested interest, although few were actively concerned in running the trust. Josiah Wedgewood was involved with many of the trusts in

Staffordshire; good roads would have aided the export of his pottery to markets in other parts of the country. In Norfolk members of the Gurney family were treasurers to many of the trusts in the county. Their involvement gave them publicity, helped to finance the trusts, and the toll receipts were a useful source of deposits to their bank, which was a forerunner of Barclays.

Each Turnpike Act was renewed every twenty-one years. Some trusts were not successful and were allowed to run down and expire, but most continued for many years, and added more roads to their jurisdiction or improved and rerouted existing roads. Most turnpike trust roads went from town A to town B, sometimes with branches to towns or villages near the main route. The West Country, however, was unique in having turnpike trusts based on one town, such as Bath, Bristol and Wells, with the toll roads radiating out like the spokes of a wheel. As will be shown later, this could cause anger to many people who were unable to find an alternative, toll-free route into the town.

Some of the earliest turnpiked roads were those leading into London and those in industrial areas such as wool routes to Barnsley and Manchester, and coal routes from Durham, Newcastle and Sunderland. They took their name from the turning of a pike, or bar, to allow the traveller access on to the road after paying his toll. Later, tollhouses were built, where the tollkeeper and his family lived. Many still survive, often distinguished by having windows placed so that the tollkeeper had a good view up and down the road (4). Some were quite elaborate buildings, circular, half-hexagonal or polygonal, while others were just humble cottages. There was sometimes an inset panel on one of the walls where a board advertising the toll charges was fixed. They had a large wooden gate or 'pike' beside them which was opened to allow travellers onto the road once they had paid the appropriate toll, and usually a small gate at the side for use by pedestrians, who did not have to pay. The charges where based on the number of animals passing through the gate and differed according to whether the traveller was on horseback or in a carriage, how many draught animals were harnessed to the vehicle, or how many beasts were in a flock or herd. Later, charges had to be added for such innovations as traction engines, and magistrates in Devon were even asked to decide whether a perambulator should be liable to tolls; they decided it should not. There were many exemptions from paying the tolls: parishioners going to church on Sundays or to a funeral, carts of manure going to improve local fields, voters going to an election, cows being taken to or from milking, soldiers on the march, and mail-coaches, to name but a few. A tollkeeper's job could not have been easy, and newspapers of the day carried many tales of fines for overcharging or embezzlement, and of robbery and murder at the turnpike gates.

There was much opposition to the toll roads, particularly from tradesmen and labourers who thought them a scheme to benefit the rich. One toll charge could be half a day's wages for

4 *Sicklesmere Tollhouse (Suffolk)*

a labourer. There were many riots, but in England they were all of a local nature and were not organised nationally. Many of the rioters disguised themselves by wearing women's clothes and blackening their faces. Between 1727 and 1749 colliers from the Forest of Dean who supplied Bristol with coal pulled down and burnt tollgates because they could find no alternative way to get into the city than by the turnpikes, and the cost of the tolls was affecting their livelihood. A graphic account in *The Gentleman's Magazine* in August 1749 tells of 700 protesters armed with rusty swords, pitchforks, axes, guns, pistols and clubs battling with sailors armed with muskets, pistols and cutlasses who had been sent to guard the turnpike gates. The Bristol Turnpike Trust was set up in 1726 and steadily incorporated the roads radiating out of Bristol. By 1799 it was the most extensive turnpike in England, covering nearly 150 miles of roads. In 1731 there were riots on the Gloucester to Hereford road, and in disturbances in Ledbury in 1735 one person was shot. In unrest in Leeds a few years later troops killed up to fifteen rioters. Parliament took a serious view of the disturbances as they considered turnpikes to be 'property', and any attacks on property were a threat to authority. From being a transportable offence, destruction of turnpike gates became a capital crime. Three of the Ledbury rioters were hanged, one of them at Tyburn. However, there was a lot of local sympathy for the rioters and juries were often unwilling to convict.[4] In Wales a century later, protesters dressed in women's clothes destroyed tollgates which had been put too close together by unscrupulous trustees intent on making a higher income. Other grievances combined to make these disturbances more serious, and they became known as the Rebecca Riots from the Biblical quotation 'And they blessed Rebecca, and said unto her, Thou art our sister, be thou the mother of thousands of millions, and let thy seed possess the gate of those which hate them' (*Genesis*, xxiv, 60). In about 1780 the tollgate at Manley, Cheshire, was burnt down, but in 1833 the trustees ordered that the tollhouse be thatched, showing that turnpikes in the region had been accepted, resistance had ceased, and that the burning down of tollgates was no longer a risk. When a new General Turnpike Act was produced in 1822 to tidy up and repeal sixteen previous Acts, the penalty for destroying a turnpike gate was once again transportation 'to One of His Majesty's Plantations Abroad for Seven Years'. There were still isolated incidences of rage against the tolls, and many letters to English newspapers pleaded with 'anyone who had any influence with Rebecca' to ask her to take up her quarters in their neighbourhood.

Businessmen could afford to employ more lawful means of protest and petitioned the House of Commons. In Sussex 'the justices of the peace, gentlemen, farmers, maltsters, grocers, owners of hop grounds, shopkeepers, stage-coachmen, waggoners, carters, carriers, fishermen, higlers [itinerant traders], and others ... whose business and affairs hourly and daily call and oblige them to go to the City of London' asked to be exempt from turnpike tolls from the Hastings area through East Grinstead and into London. There were other reasons for disapproval. The Hon. John Byng wished that 'half the turnpike roads in the kingdom were plough'd up, which have imported London manners, and depopulated the country'. William Cobbett was another traveller who disliked the turnpikes. He avoided them so that he could observe the genuine life of the countryside.

There is no doubt that the turnpike roads benefited the country. Manufactured goods could be transported to the main population centres, and farm produce could be taken to market more quickly and efficiently, although livestock was usually taken by other routes to avoid the tolls, to use roads with softer surfaces to prevent damage to the animals' feet, and to provide grazing along the way. Wheeled traffic began to increase, and the 1750s saw the introduction of stage-coaches which speeded passenger traffic and the carrying of the mails. In most cases the turnpikes used existing roads, often improving them for wheeled traffic by straightening bends and avoiding steep gradients. As England became more industrialised, however, new roads were built to serve the growing manufacturing towns and link them with the markets and suppliers.

Trust development tended to follow the fluctuations in trade and industry. 'Turnpike Mania' lasted from 1751 to 1772, a time of economic growth, when 389 trusts were established. By the mid-nineteenth century there were over one thousand turnpikes, many of the earlier ones having been extended or amalgamated. A list of the turnpike roads created in England and Wales, with the Act of Parliament setting them up, can be found in William Albert's book *The Turnpike Road System in*

England 1663-1840 (see Bibliography). By the 1840s railways were rapidly taking over long-distance traffic. Trust toll receipts fell, and it became harder to raise enough money for road repairs. A report of a meeting of turnpike trustees in the *Cambridge Chronicle and Journal* on 3 June 1848 casts a note of despair. They had been unable to let the tolls on the Ely to Downham Market road because of their depreciation by the railways. They had given up possession of the tolls to the mortgagees and 'by this proceeding they have placed themselves in a dilemma, as to be without funds they might as well be defunct'. Gradually the turnpike trusts were wound up, and the roads were 'disturnpiked', the last trust disappearing in 1895. When the turnpike trusts were wound up, property such as tollhouses, water pumps and carts, and fencing was sold, but the milestones were left for the continuing benefit of travellers. The tollhouses became private dwellings, and, sadly, many have since been demolished. Some of the tollboards are now in museums, but a few have survived *in situ*. One can be seen at Butterrow Toll House, Rodborough (Glos.). Another board is still fixed to the tollhouse on the former Todmorden to Littleborough turnpike (Yorks.).

The science of road building at this time was poor and, in many cases, roads were not significantly improved when they became turnpikes. It was thought that wear and tear on the road surface could be reduced by changing the design of vehicles and, therefore, higher tolls were charged for wagons with narrow wheel treads, or felloes. However, John Loudon Macadam pointed out that too much attention was being paid to vehicles and not enough to road construction. From the late 1750s, John Metcalfe (known as Blind Jack of Knaresborough), despite having lost his sight at the age of six as a result of smallpox and having had no special engineering training, experimented with new road surfaces on many Yorkshire turnpikes, and in the early nineteenth century Macadam and Thomas Telford developed new methods of road construction which greatly speeded traffic and formed the basis for our modern highways.

It was the turnpike era that saw the greatest increase in milestones. From the 1740s Turnpike Acts began to stipulate that milestones should be erected along the road and the General Turnpike Act of 1767 made them compulsory.[5] 'And, for the better Convenience of Travellers', it read, '... the Commissioners or Trustees appointed ... shall direct the Surveyor of every such Turnpike Road ... to erect Mile-stones upon such Turnpike Road, with proper Inscriptions and Figures thereupon, denoting the Names and Distances from the principal Towns or Places on each respective Road.' Surveyors who neglected their duty were fined £1. Accurately measured roads with distance markers were also a great help to the expanding

network of mail-coaches whose drivers had strict timetables to keep and no speedometers to tell them how fast they were travelling. Many milestones still to be seen in Yorkshire conveniently show the turnpike name. All are made of cast iron with a backing stone and date from about 1825. Good examples can be found near Ingleton (Lancaster & Richmond Road, turnpiked 1751), Bramham - in a layby off the south-bound carriageway of the A1 - (Ferrybridge & Boroughbridge Road, turnpiked 1741), Long Preston (Keighley & Kendal Road, turnpiked 1753), Skipton (Skipton & Knaresborough Road, turnpiked 1771), Grangemoor (Barnsley & Grangemoor Road, turnpiked 1759) (**5**) and Frostrow - in Cumbria since 1974 - (Sedburgh & Hawes Road, turnpiked 1761). Many varied examples of

5 Grangemoor (Yorks.)

milestones still remain, details of which are given in Chapters 4, 5 and 6.

Only a very small proportion of the roads in England were brought under the turnpike system, and private individuals continued to pay for milestones, as can be seen from some acrimonious correspondence between William Tooke of Thompson and Thomas de Grey (Lord Walsingham) of Merton, Norfolk in 1772. Tooke and five labourers had destroyed gates, fences and trees on de Grey's estate which they said obstructed the old Thetford to Watton road, causing travellers to go across Tooke's land, much to his annoyance. If de Grey replaced the obstructions in the same place, Tooke 'wood cut through all the plantations and fences ware old Roads had bin'. He threatened that if de Grey did not 'soon replace the Mile Stones and Posts, in the Thetford Road, and the Gate at Ganes Lane, I will remove every Gate which he has put up illegally on the Highways ... To this I do not want any answer, *but it shall be done*.' The reply stated that 'the Mile Stones from Thetford are Mr de Grey's Property being placed there at his sole expence. The Gate at the end of Gaines Lane had been broken so many times, and so often repaired by Mr de Grey, that he was tired of the trouble and expence.' The dispute over the route of this road lasted several years, culminating in a challenge to a duel and a court case. A turnpike was later proposed between Thetford and Watton, but was opposed by Lord Walsingham because it would have damaged his rabbit warrens. Lord Walsingham's milestones no longer exist, but many others put up privately by landowners are still in place, and examples are given in later chapters.

Packhorse and Drove Roads

For centuries the packhorse had been the main means of transporting goods. In lowland areas they were gradually superseded by wagons, but in hill country, especially in the Pennines, packhorses remained in use well into the nineteenth century. Strings of up to forty horses would be attended by two or three men. The horses had bells on their harness to warn of their approach on the steep, narrow tracks. Sturdy horses of Scottish descent called galloways were often used. The legacy of the packhorse trains is still widespread in Yorkshire and Derbyshire, and is to be found in place and road names derived from such traders as 'salters' (salt dealers), 'badgers' or 'swailers' (corn dealers), and 'broggers' (wool dealers) who transported these goods across the high moorland on horseback, or in variations of 'hollow way' to describe the tracks eroded by traffic and rain to a lower level than the surrounding land.

Travellers who were strangers to the area, such as Celia Fiennes and Daniel Defoe, needed guides when crossing the Peak District, and there are many cases of people dying after becoming lost on the moors. Cairns, stone slabs, stone crosses or wooden posts were erected on many tracks, and in 1697 an Act of Parliament authorised local Justices of the Peace to direct highway surveyors to put up a stone or post 'for the better convenience of travelling in such Parts of this Kingdome which are remote from Towns and where several High-ways meet'.[6] These guide stones, stoops or moorstones were usually square pillars of roughly cut stone, and had to give the names of the nearest market towns, and sometimes had hands carved to point the way. Most, however, assumed that the traveller turned right from the face showing his destination. Some of the guide stones on Dartmoor just have a large capital letter to represent the town. The square granite pillar at Cross Furzes shows B, A and T on different sides, standing for Brent, Ashburton and Tavistock. Celia Fiennes was enthusiastic about guide stones. Writing of her travels in Lancashire in 1698 she says: 'they have one good thing in most parts of this principality ... that at all cross wayes there are Posts with Hands pointing to each road with the names of the great towns or market towns that it leads to, which does make up for the length of the miles that strangers may not loose their road and have it to goe back again ...' Some highway surveyors were slow to implement the order to put up guide stones, and the local Justices had to repeat the order every few years, threatening a fine if the Act was not complied with. Many of the stones bear a date which usually coincides with a reminder made at the Quarter Sessions. An example from Derbyshire can be found near Ball Cross on the Bakewell to Edensor road which is inscribed 'Sheffield Rode; Chesterfield Rode; Bakewell Rode'. It also has hands to point the way, and the date 1709. Another stone in Longshaw Park near Sheffield needs some imagination to interpret, the narrowness of the stone requiring frequent breaks in the inscription (indicated here by an oblique line): 'TO HA/THAR/SICH/ANDSº/TO CH/APIL I/N Lee/ FRITH TO/SHAFILD/1709 TO/TIDS/WEL TO/CHAS/TER/ FILD'. Surveyors in the West Riding of Yorkshire were even more tardy and from the 1730s Quarter Session Order Books show repeated reminders. From 1738 the orders state that distances should be shown on guide stones, and many stones

found in the West Riding do show the mileage, and are often dated from this time. Guide stones without mileages can also be found in Cornwall. A line of granite posts can be traced north from St Germans, that at Halwinnick Butts showing 'CAM/EL/FOR/DE; RED/ GAT/E; LIS/KEA/RD; LAU/ N/ CES/ TON', one name on each of the four sides of the stone. A more elaborate post with carved hands pointing the way can be seen near Stoke Climsland (6).

The eighteenth and early nineteenth centuries saw the golden age of the drover. The industrial revolution had

6 *Stoke Climsland (Cornwall)*

lured many people to jobs in towns and they needed to be fed. The Napoleonic War also created a need for salt meat for the army and navy. The best areas of Britain for raising cattle and sheep were Scotland and Wales, and every year hundreds of thousands of beasts were driven to markets in England. Some were sold directly to butchers, others were fattened first in areas such as the coastal grazing marshes of Norfolk. The drovers tried to avoid the turnpikes, mainly because of the expense of the tolls. It could also increase the journey time when only one animal at a time could pass through the tollgate to ease counting. Although many of the cattle were shod, the drovers preferred to find softer paths for their animals and also routes which provided grazing along the way. Many prehistoric tracks and Roman roads were used by the drovers as well as some of the packhorse trails.

Fairs were established in places such as York, Huntingdon, and St Faiths (Norfolk) where the beasts were bought and sold, the ultimate destination for many being Smithfield in London. Like the packhorse routes, many of the drove roads can still be traced by associated names. Bullock Hill and Calf Lane in Horsham St Faith (Norfolk) are reminders of the great livestock fair, the site of which is now covered with houses. The Welsh Road, one of the main droving routes for cattle coming from Wales, can still be traced through Warwickshire. Inn names can give a clue, such as The Black Bull, The Drover's Arms, The Scotsman's Pack (many drovers were Scottish).

One of the droving routes from Scotland came via Carter Bar, Corbridge, Northallerton, Thirsk and Easingwold to the fair at York. In Ingramgate, Thirsk (Yorks.) stands a triangular-plan, cast iron milepost which was made at a nearby foundry in Norby. On one side of the post a drover has been painted carrying his cattle prod and a mug of beer, for which the town was also renowned. On the other face are two bullocks. As the animals approached London from the north, many congregated at Barnet where another fair was held. From there the route came through Highgate, St Giles, Holborn and thence to Smithfield. A fine stone pillar near an old inn called 'The Flask' in Highgate marks 'IV/Miles/from Saint/Giles Pound'. Highgate taverns were reputed to be the final stopping places for the drovers before reaching their ultimate destination, and the custom of 'swearing on the horns' took place in these establishments, strangers having to swear an oath on a set of horns tied to a pole then buying drinks in order to be allowed to stay. Across the heath in Hampstead another milestone from the droving era records $3^{1}/_{2}$ miles to St Giles's Pound and 4 miles to Holborn Bars. The drove route from the north met that from the west near the church of St Giles-in-the-Fields, and the pound was probably where stray animals were penned until a fine secured their release. By the mid-eighteenth century this area was a squalid slum, and with the annual passage of tens of thousands of cattle, sheep, pigs and donkeys, conditions must have been indescribable.

Parish and Town Roads

Only about one-sixth of the roads in England were ever turnpiked, the other five-sixths remaining under the jurisdiction of the parish or town. Parliament tried many times to introduce a rate to cover road maintenance, but this was so unpopular that the system of Statute Labour brought in in 1555 continued with little change until the mid-nineteenth century. The parish vestry chose a highway surveyor - sometimes called a waywarden, boonmaster or stoneman - who was often a local farmer, and who usually knew nothing about road repair. From the early 1800s the able-bodied paupers of the parish were used as the labour force, and paid a pittance for their work. The system was, needless to say, very inefficient. Under the General Highway Act of 1835, the vestry was given the power to levy a rate and appoint a salaried surveyor, but the areas of jurisdiction were not large enough to give economy in purchasing materials and labour or to attract efficient professional surveyors. Later in the nineteenth century, some parishes joined together to administer roads running through them, and in some cases erected a series of milestones on these roads.

Roads in towns and cities were administered by the Corporations, and Boards of Commissioners were appointed to carry out such improvements as paving and lighting streets, building and repairing bridges, and clearing all manner of filth and rubbish from the highways. They sometimes put up milestones. In 1848 urban roads came under the control of the Local Boards of Health, and in 1862 an attempt was made to combine parish roads into Highway Districts under Highway Boards. The Local Government Act of 1894 established Urban and Rural District Councils based on the former Sanitary Authorities and they took over responsibility for most minor roads. It is probable that some of these new councils erected milestones, but evidence is not easy to find. A triangular, cast iron post at Bacton on the Peterchurch to Pontrilas road (Her. & Worcs.) reads 'DORE RURAL DISTRICT' at the top. Under the Local Government Act of 1929, responsibility for maintaining rural roads eventually passed to the County Councils.

The Twentieth Century

The county councils were established in 1888 and were obliged to take over and maintain the former turnpikes. They also had

the power to add other roads to their jurisdiction which they deemed to be main roads. Some county councils were more conscientious than others on road maintenance, and even put up their own milestones. A large number survive in Cheshire, all of the same style, a good example being found on the A483 on the outskirts of Chester. A cast iron, V-plan milepost reads 'CHESHIRE COUNTY COUNCIL 1898' on its top face, while similar ones at

7 *Waverton (Cheshire)*

Audlem and Waverton are dated 1896 (**7**). Several county council posts survive in Somerset dated between 1909 and

29

1913, that near Shepton Mallet on the A371 dated 1909 being a good example. The only complete cast iron milepost left in Nottinghamshire is on the A60 at Oldcotes, and reads 'N.C.C.' at the top. A cast iron milepost in Lincolnshire, on the Boston road near the Bicker Bar roundabout, bears the initials 'HCC' at the top. Some counties were considered too large and were therefore subdivided for administrative purposes. Yorkshire was divided into three ridings - North, East and West - Sussex into East and West, and Lincolnshire had three administrative areas - Holland, Kesteven and Lindsey, which explains the 'HCC' on the milepost. Holland County Council survived until 1974. Another reminder of these divisions is a milepost on the outskirts of Richmond (Yorks.) with 'NRYCC' cast on the upper face - North Riding of Yorkshire County Council. One of the best areas for finding county council milestones is Norfolk. They are mostly of triangular pattern, but variations seem to coincide with the highway districts into which the county was divided. All read 'N.C.C. MAIN ROAD'. Concrete posts on the A140 between Norwich and Cromer filled the gaps where turnpike trust milestones were missing. Stones stand along the A149 between Great Yarmouth and North Walsham. This road was never a turnpike, but must have been deemed a busy road in need of council attention. At Burgh St Margaret and Filby stand cast iron posts made in the early twentieth century. The A1064 which passes them became the Norwich to Gt Yarmouth Turnpike in 1769, but this winding eastern half of the route was superseded by the 'Acle Straight' (now the A47) in 1831, shortening the route by three and a half miles. The fledgling County Council must have thought it worth while to fill the gaps in the turnpike milestones on the old road. Milestones of other patterns can be seen near Billingford on the B1145 to King's Lynn (not previously turnpiked although it was a major coach route), and on the A1122 east of Downham Market near Crimplesham (turnpiked in 1772). The county councils were divided into highway districts for the purposes of road maintenance, and this is reflected in some cast iron posts in Yorkshire. At Swinithwaite, on the former Lancaster to

Richmond Turnpike, the V-plan post shows 'LEYBURN H.D' on the upper face **(8)**; a similar post at Sedbusk, once on the Sedbergh to Askrigg Turnpike, shows 'ASKRIGG H.D'. As late as the 1930s, Worcestershire County Council replaced some of its missing milestones, (e.g. on the A44). The concrete posts, shaped rather like a slice through a mushroom, have metal plates for the mileage and for the road number and were designed by the deputy surveyor Mr Brook Bradley.

8 *Swinithwaite (Yorks.)*

The advent of railways caused a decline in road traffic in the mid-nineteenth century but a resurgence in the use of roads began towards the end of the century, first with the invention of bicycles, then the internal combustion engine. By 1906 over 45,000 motor vehicles were licensed, and by 1914 the number had risen to nearly 389,000. Road signs began to appear in the late nineteenth century when the Bicycle Union put up warning notices of steep hills and sharp bends.[7] After 1903 local authorities began to erect road signs, and later the Automobile Association and Royal Automobile Club put up signs of their own design. In the 1920s the AA installed place names at the entrance to towns and villages. The yellow and black metal disks had the name of the place with mileages to two or three other towns along the road, and usually also the distance to London **(9)**. A few of these disks have survived *in situ* and others can be seen in museums. It was not until 1933 that the designs for road signs were standardised. In 1964 regulations were passed to bring British road signs into line with those in Europe where signs were predominantly pictorial with little or

31

no wording. In 1922 the Ministry of Transport (which had been established two years earlier) started the modern system of route numbering. London was taken as the hub and the main roads from the capital were numbered radiating clockwise, creating the A1 (Great North Road), A2 (Dover road), A3 (Portsmouth road) etc. County councils took over responsibility for all roads in 1929 because the burden of maintenance was becoming too heavy for the urban and rural district councils, and a few years later the Ministry of Transport took the main trunk roads under its wing.

At the end of May 1940, the Transport Minister, Sir John Reith, announced in Parliament that highway authorities had been instructed to remove all signposts and direction signs that might aid an enemy in the event of invasion. It was later realised that milestones could also help the enemy find his whereabouts, and it was ordered that they should be taken up and hidden, or defaced. Although it is likely that many milestones were left untouched, particularly in areas where the danger of invasion was thought not to be serious, the orders were complied with in many parts of the country. Some were taken to council depots, a few had their lettering filled with cement. Many of them were buried close to where they had stood. Those that could not be uprooted, perhaps if they were set in a pavement, had the inscription chiselled away. Many milestones can be found today with bolt holes where a metal plate was once fixed to them, the metal probably having been melted down to help the war effort. Some of the guide stones in the Pennines were used for target

9 Bedingfield (Suffolk)

practice by the Home Guard. Although many were re-instated, a large number of milestones were sadly lost at this time. In at least one case (Norwich) the council depot in which they were stored was destroyed by bombing, and some milestones were later sacrificed for use in post-war rebuilding. Some still rest where they were buried and there are regular reports of them being unearthed.

Post-war road development has been one of constant change, the era of the by-pass and the motorway. Modern standardised road signs have little character and hardly warrant a second glance. The modern equivalent of milestones are the emergency telephones on motorways, one mile apart.

Conclusion

Apart from the modern era of road building, there have only been two other periods in our history when roads were created artificially - the Roman occupation and the age of the turnpike. These were also times of more central administration of highways, and saw the main bloom of milestones along our roads. The twentieth century has seen more changes to the English road network than has occurred throughout the rest of our history. Many of the main coaching roads of the past are now 'B' roads, minor country lanes, or even cross-country tracks, while prehistoric ridgeways, droveways and packhorse trails are being turned into long-distance footpaths. There are still many clues, however, to their former use if we look at the names of roads, settlements, buildings and landmarks, and investigate archaeological remains such as ancient settlements, evidence of Roman occupation, monastic estates, coaching inns, tollhouses and milestones. With over 19,000 miles of turnpike roads in England by the 1830s, there must have been a great profusion of milestones associated with them, not to mention many set up by towns, parishes and individuals. It is impossible to say how many remain today. A few county industrial archaeology societies, and some individuals, are trying to locate those that still exist in their areas, and a small number are safe in museums. It is to be hoped that an increasing interest in them will lead to the preservation of those that are left. As is shown in later chapters, milestones are still being made, and they can be just as interesting or eccentric as those of the past, and far more worthy of notice than modern standardised road signs.

CHAPTER 3

Miles, Measurement and Maps

The Mile

The name 'mile' comes from the Roman *milia passuum* which was one thousand paces of a runner's stride of five feet. The Roman mile measured approximately 1,620 yds (1,482 m). Although road distances in Roman Britain used this length, it was by no means always the case in other parts of the Roman Empire, where local measurements were often used. An African mile measured 1,777 yds (1,625 m) and the Gallic league approximately 2,625 yds (2,400 m). It is thought that British Imperial linear measurements were later derived from those in use in Roman Gaul. The division of the English mile into eight furlongs may have been based on the eight subdivisions, or *stadia* of the Roman mile. The word furlong is derived from 'furrow long', a convenient ploughing distance. The yard measurement seems to have remained unchanged for many centuries, so that this can be used as a criterion for calculating the length of the different mile measurements that have been used since Roman times.

Fynes Moryson wrote a section in his *Itinerary* of 1617 under the heading 'Of the divers measures of miles, through divers parts of the world', in which he states that 'five Italian miles, or three French, or two and a halfe English, make one Dutch mile, and that one Dutch mile and a halfe makes a mile of Sweitzerland'.[1] He was of the opinion that the miles near London were generally shorter, 'but towards the North, & in some particular places of England, the miles are longer, among which the Kentish mile ... is proverbially held to be

35

extraordinarily long ...' 'This I am sure of the more I travell'd northward the longer I found the miles, I am sure these 6 miles and the other 6 miles to Haltwhistle might with modesty be esteemed double the number in most of the countys of England; I did not go 2 of those miles in an hour ...' wrote Celia Fiennes in 1698. In September 1726 Henry Curwen rode from Workington to London and wrote, in a wonderfully unpunctuated account of one day's journey through Yorkshire, that he 'stopt at Greata Bridge and Drank 2 Muggs of ale Lay at the Bull Katricd Lane Rid 32 miles this day near 50 Mesurd Miles Bad Road'.

English Linear Measurement

Imperial	Yards (yds)	Metric Metres (m)
3 feet	1	0.9144
1 rod/pole/perch	5^1/$_2$	5.0292
1 chain	22	20.1168
40 poles=10 chains = 1 furlong	220	201.168
8 furlongs = 1mile	1,760	1609.344

Note: To avoid confusion, and because milestones were erected in the days of yards, furlongs, miles etc., most distances in the text have been given in Imperial measurement. To convert Imperial to metric, multiply yards by 0.9144 to get the distance in metres.

From the study of distances on maps of the fourteenth, fifteenth and sixteenth centuries, it is clear that a great variety of mile measurements were used, with the average containing over ten furlongs (2,012 yds, or 1,840 m).[2]

The first legislation on mileage did not occur until 1593 when a Statute was passed by Parliament to stop any new buildings being erected 'in London, Westminster, or three miles thereof'.[3] It concluded that 'a mile shall contain 8 furlongs, every furlong 40 poles, and every pole shall contain 16 foot and an halfe.' Thus was born the statute mile of 1,760 yds (1,609 m), but only in London! Apart from the widely used customary mile of approximately 2,428 yds (2,220 m), other parts of the kingdom used a great variety of measurements; a Welsh mile was about 2,508 yds (2,293 m), an Irish mile 2,240 yds (2,048 m), and a Scottish mile 1,976 yds (1,807 m). Often three different scales were given. According to Plot's *Natural History of Oxfordshire* (1677) that county had greater, less and middle miles, with the latter containing 2,035 yds (1,861 m). Kent had long, little and good miles, and also great, middle and small miles, while Saxton's map of England (1583) gives the mileage scales of magna, mediocria and parva. The terms computed, customary and common miles were also widely used. The miles in Kent were acknowledged to be some of the longest in the country, and those who hired out horses took advantage of this by charging 3d. (lp) a mile to compensate for the extra distance. This was ^{1}/2d. a mile more than the standard rate. In 1633 the Dover postmaster had the road measured as far as Canterbury and had markers put at every statute mile, but continued to charge 3d. a mile for horse hire. This resulted in complaints to Parliament (see also Chapter 2).

The statute mile was used by John Ogilby, who produced the first accurate road maps of England in the late seventeenth century. Details of his work are given in a later section of this chapter. Ogilby gives three sets of mileages between main towns. Those between London and Holyhead are as follows:

direct horizontal distance	224 miles
vulgar computation	208 miles
measured miles	269^1/2 miles

He explains direct horizontal distance as that measured by latitude and longitude, vulgar computation as 'vulgar belief', and the last as measured in statute miles by a surveyor's wheel.

The old English or customary mile of about 2,428 yds (2,220 m) continued to be used for some time, even until the nineteenth century in the north of England. When guide stones were erected in the West Riding of Yorkshire in the eighteenth century, many used the customary mile to record distances (see also Chapter 2). John Brigg recorded at least seventy-five of these stones before World War II.[4] Some of these customary milestones, originally set up between about 1700 and 1790, still remain today. Two survivors can be found near Todmorden, one showing Burnley 9 miles, Todmorden 2 miles, Rochdale 5 miles and Halifax 10 miles. The distances in statute miles, according to Brigg, are $11^3/_4$, $2^2/_3$, $6^1/_2$ and 14 respectively. The other stone, near the Shepherd's Rest, Todmorden, gives Burnley 7 miles, Rochdale 6 miles and Halifax 9 miles (10, $8^1/_2$ and 12 statute miles respectively). Brigg also recorded a stone which still stands near Longridge in the Hodder Valley, now in Lancashire. It is dated 1766 and bears the initials IS. Its distances are Lancaster 16, Preston 10, Whalley 3 and Gisburn 8 (20, $15^1/_2$, $4^1/_2$ and $10^1/_2$ statute miles). In Brigg's article of 1914, a tall, slender stone dated 1739 near Dunsop Bridge is described. Its inscription is as follows: 'TO/CLIT/HERO/7 Ms; To/ LANK/ STER/ 11 Ms; To/ HORN/ BY 10/ Ms; To/ SLAD/BVRN/M 3'. The article mentions a 'modern' iron signpost set into the top of the old milestone, with the statute miles marked as Clitheroe 11, Lancaster 15 and Slaidburn 5. The road to Hornby had disappeared by then but would have been 13 statute miles. A very modern signpost now stands beside these markers, and has reduced the distance to Slaidburn to 4 miles. As some guide stones recorded statute rather than customary miles, travellers must have been thoroughly confused. A guide stone near Tebay, formerly in the West Riding of Yorkshire but in Cumbria since 1974, has the distances Orton 7 miles and Sedbergh 2 miles inscribed on it. The first mileage is correct in statute miles, but Sedbergh is about 4 statute miles away.

The Post Office adopted the statute mile after its foundation in 1649 for determining the charges for hiring post-horses, and when turnpike trust surveyors began setting up milestones they also used the measurement. It was not until the

Uniform Weights and Measures Act was passed in 1824 that the 1,760 yard mile was established throughout the country. The Act was needed to stop 'great confusion and manifest frauds'.[5] A standard yard measure was kept in the House of Commons, and consisted of a brass rod with two golden studs. The yard was measured as the distance between the centre point of each stud 'the brass being at the temperature of sixty-two degrees by Fahrenheit's thermometer'. These standard measures were made available to the public by being set into the walls of public buildings to enable workmen to check their tools. One of the best places to see them is in a wall outside the Old Royal Observatory, Greenwich.

A few milestones can be found which give other measurements besides miles (**10,11,26**). Cornwall has several

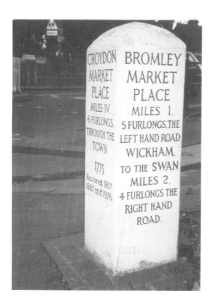

10 *Beckenham (London)*   **11** *Moretonhampstead (Devon)*

examples. A stone at Trerulefoot, with a heavily abbreviated inscription, gives the miles, poles and yards thus: '7M/22P/lY/S/B'. The SB probably refers to Saltash steam bridge. A granite stone by a parapet of the bridge at Bearland gives the distance to Callington as 'C/6 Furlongs/2 Poles', while on the A390 a tall stone shows '4^1/$_3$/ furlongs to Callington/market gate/L8'. A small stone opposite the entrance to Gresham's School in Norfolk tells us it is 3^1/$_2$ furlongs to the nearby town of Holt. Near Ashcombe (Devon) the distance to Exeter on the milestone near the junction of the B3192 with the A380 is given in miles, furlongs and poles. The fine obelisk in Southwark (London) **(37)** gives 'ONE MILE/XXXX FEET/FROM LONDON BRIDGE' (see also Chapter 5), while an equally precise stone in Helmshore (Lancs.) announces 1^3/$_4$ miles 255 yards to Haslingden.

The Measurement of Roads
<u>Measuring</u> Instruments

Surprisingly good results were achieved by the early surveyors using very basic techniques. Alfred Watkins, in his theory of ley lines, surmised that pre-Roman Britons created their straight tracks with sighting staves, the Long Man of Wilmington in Sussex being possibly a representation of one of these early surveyors. He suggested that the 'staff of office' derives from the tools of the trade of this important profession. Whether this is true or not, we can be sure, however, that the Romans used sighting staves, and measuring rods marked in feet to determine distances. There were attempts to produce more sophisticated instruments, and Vitruvius gives very precise instructions for constructing a primitive kind of mileometer called a hodometer which could be built into a carriage.[6] The wheels had to be four Roman feet in diameter with a drum fastened to the inner side of the hub. A tooth on this drum engaged with four hundred teeth on a drum above, with one larger tooth engaging with a third drum which dropped a small pebble into a bronze vessel at each turn. The traveller could tell by the ringing of the stone falling into the pot that he had covered a mile, and at the end of his journey could count the stones to determine his total distance.

After the Roman period there was little need for measuring roads for many centuries, and when English surveying textbooks began to be published in the sixteenth century, the writers had to draw their material from the Continent. Most length measurements were achieved using simple poles, or ropes with knots at determined intervals. In the early seventeenth century the measuring chain came into use. Gunter's chain was the most widely employed, sixty-six feet long divided into one hundred links.[7] This gave its name to the measurement of a chain (66 ft or 22 yds - see table in previous section). The chain was a cheap, simple measuring instrument and was widely used for many centuries, especially for estate maps where the high cost of more sophisticated instruments was unacceptable and unnecessary. When Dr William Warren was preparing to place milestones on the road from Cambridge in 1725 he wrote: 'I took two men along with me, & with a Chain of 66 feet in Length we measur'd five miles from the Southwest Buttress of Great St Maries Church Steeple in Cambridge towards Barkway' (see Chapter 4 for more details).[8] The landscape architect Humphry Repton noted in his account book in 1789 the purchase of a Gunter's chain for 8s. 6d. (42p).

The surveyor's wheel was in use by the seventeenth century. It consisted of an iron-shod wheel, usually with a circumference of sixteen and a half feet with a dial below the handle which recorded the distance in poles, furlongs and miles. The wheel was pushed along by the surveyor. It was a quick and easy method, but was said to have the disadvantage of over-estimating the distance because it went down hollows and over hillocks. It went by many names: perambulator, dimensurator, and waywiser, the latter name derived from the German *weg weiser* meaning to show the way. In 1657 John Evelyn wrote of visiting Colonel Blount, who showed him 'the application of the way-wiser to a coach, exactly measuring the miles, and showing them by an index as we went on. It had three circles, one pointing to the number of rods, another to the miles, by 10 to 1000, with all the subdivisions of quarters; very pretty and useful.' John Ogilby was very enthusiastic about this technique, saying in the introduction to *Britannia* that he had been 'much facilitated in this Great work by the wheel Dimensurator, which, for Ease and Accurateness infinitely surpasses the Chain, as being manageable by a Single Person ... We readily acknowledge, and even in wheels themselves, commend rather the Foot-Wheel ... than any such like Coach or Chariot-Mensurator whatsoever'. A modern version of the surveyor's wheel is still used today.

Datum Points

Roman datum points on which measurements from a principal city were based, such as the Golden Milestone in Rome and the London Stone, have already been mentioned in Chapter 2. In more recent times, many varied datum points have been used. A round bronze plaque in the south-west buttress of Gt St Mary's Church in Cambridge marks the place from whence Dr Warren started measuring the road to Barkway in 1725. Up to about 1865, a milestone outside the White Lion Hotel in the market-place in Chester was used to measure the coaching roads out of that city. When the area was rebuilt a few years later, the stone disappeared, and the High Cross took over the function. Roads from Liverpool were measured from the Corn Exchange.

A correspondent to the *Eastern Daily Press* in 1909 wondered whether milestones giving distances to Norwich meant to the Guildhall or to the nearest city gate. Someone went to the trouble of measuring the ten former turnpikes radiating from the city and found that in almost every case, the first milestone was one mile from the nearest city gate.

Some milestones conveniently give the precise place from which they were measured (**10**). Terminus posts on the network of turnpikes leading into Bath show the number of miles and furlongs to the Guildhall, the post north of Stratton-on-the-Fosse (Somerset) being a good example. Milestones around Liskeard (Cornwall) show that a variety of datum points were used in just one town. A stone on the A38 to Torpoint reads '^{1}/2 mile to the Church Gates', while another on the Callington road at Hendrabridge reads '1 mile from Centre of Parade'. A stone on the Lostwithiel road announces that it is half a mile to the cross in Church Street. A similar datum point is recorded on a stone in Bromfield (Salop) which shows 3 miles to Ludlow Cross. A cast iron post in Rotherham (Yorks.) with very precise datum points can be found 1 mile from College Square, $22^1/4$ from Mansfield Town Hall, $19^1/4$ from Pleasley Old Cross and $11^3/4$ from Clown Old Cross. Town halls also feature on a milestone at Cabus (Lancs.) - those of Lancaster and Garstang. Warminster Town Hall provides the measuring point for a cast iron post in Tytherington (Wilts.) **(34)**. The cattle market at Thrapston (Northants) provides the datum point for a small milestone 5 furlongs away on the Oundle road, and Frome Market House is mentioned on a cast iron post half a mile away on the Bath road in Somerset. The cast iron milepost in the High Street in Gorleston (Norfolk) is dated 1818 and may be unique in giving the mileage to what could be considered a tourist attraction - Nelson's Monument **(29)**. The 144 ft high column topped by a statue of Britannia was built in Great Yarmouth in 1817 and is one foot shorter and twenty-two years earlier than Nelson's Column in London.

River crossings were also focal points for starting measurements. Nine miles to Chippenham Bridge is shown on a milestone at Marshfield (Glos.), and a stone at Bramerton (Norfolk) shows 6 miles to Buckenham Ferry, which once crossed the river Yare east of Norwich. A later mode of transport is recorded by a cast iron post near Leamington Spa (Warwicks.) showing a quarter of a mile from Harbury Station **(12)**. The road was turnpiked in 1852 specifically to serve the station. The railway line has survived, along with Station Road and the Great Western Hotel, but the station has long since disappeared. On the bridge taking the A50 over the river at Burton on Trent (Staffs.) a narrow cast iron plaque reads 'M.R. STATION BURTON 1 MILE', referring to the Midland Railway station, which has also been demolished. A very precise stone at Bramhope (Yorks.) gives distances in miles and furlongs to two churches, two halls, a school, a station, and a bridge.

With the increasing sophistication of mail services, post offices assumed an important place in town centres. It is surprising, therefore, that these seldom feature as a datum point. In north London a milestone at Haverstock Hill records 4 miles

from the Post Office, corresponding to the distance from the General Post Office which stood in St Martin's-le-Grand from 1829 until 1912. The nightly departure of the mail-coaches was one of the sights of London. Postal charges were calculated on mileage from St Martin's to another post town along a mail-coach route, and as most roads were still measured from their traditional datum points, the distance from that point to St Martin's was added. Prior to the building of the General Post Office at St Martin's, the depot had been in Lombard Street, and postal charges were then calculated from The Standard in Cornhill. In 1840 the uniform penny post was introduced, the charge covering carriage between and delivery within post towns. Not until 1900 was the service extended to guarantee delivery throughout Britain. Several small metal posts in Darlington (Co. Durham) show distances of one mile or one and a half miles to the GPO. Local postal historians think the posts may have been used in the late nineteenth century to determine the charges for delivering telegrams or express letters. Ten posts were shown on a late-nineteenth-century town map. Of these, five are still *in situ* and a sixth is in Darlington Museum.

12 *Harbury (Warwicks.)*

London, however, must beat all records for the number of different datum points. 'At present every road begins its measurement from a different point' bemoaned a correspondent to *The Gentleman's Magazine* in 1778. He recommended that a stone pillar then standing at the intersection of Fleet Street, Ludgate, Fleet Ditch and Fleet-market should be 'considered as the centre of all the British roads' so that someone making a journey via the capital would know the exact distance he had to go. He had good cause for complaint, and confusion. Many of these datum points are recorded on milestones. Most of the stones mentioned below are described in more detail elsewhere, and the Gazetteer should be consulted for further information.

Roads into London were some of the first to be turnpiked in the early eighteenth century. Routes going south-east into Kent were generally measured from London Bridge (probably the southern end). Stone posts with metal plates can still be found on the former New Cross Turnpike. From its inception in 1718, it gradually extended its network of roads from The Borough to Dartford, Foots Cray, Farnborough and Croydon. A milestone standing in Foots Cray Road, Eltham gives 9 miles to London Bridge. Other milestones showing this destination can be seen at Avery Hill in Eltham, and Beckenham (London) (**10**), Dartford Road, Bexley and High Street, Canterbury (Kent) (**3**).

After its opening in 1750, Westminster Bridge formed the starting point for roads to Sussex. Stones at Sheffield Park and Lewes (Sussex) show this datum, as does the 'White Lady' at Esher (Surrey) (**40**). A square stone pillar at Claremont Park, Esher shows the distance to The Standard in Cornhill on the front face with the date 1747 underneath. On one of the side faces it shows 16³/4 miles from Westminster Bridge above the date 1768. The latter inscription must have been added to the stone after the opening of the bridge.

One of the busiest entrances to the capital was the tollgate at Hyde Park Corner in the settlements of Kensington and Knightsbridge. It formed the starting point for roads going in more westerly directions and this datum point can be found on milestones in Knightsbridge, and Barnes Common (London) (**13**) (1 and 5 miles respectively), Burntcommon (Surrey) (23 miles), Knowl Hill (Berks.) (30 miles), Box (Wilts.) (100 miles), Chipping Sodbury (Glos.) (108 miles) and Dorchester (Dorset) (120 miles).

The most important datum point in London, however, was The Standard in Cornhill. John Ogilby compared it to the Golden Milestone in Rome and used it as the starting point for measuring the main highways out of London in his road book  *Britannia*, published in 1675. The Standard was a large water conduit situated at the junction of Cornhill, Gracechurch Street, Bishopsgate Street and Leadenhall Street. It was first erected in the late fourteenth century and was fed with waste water for cleaning the streets. After 1603 it was no longer in use and was eventually removed about 1674. However, it had been such a prominent landmark that its former position was used as a measuring point for many years afterwards. Several milestones in Surrey give a distance from

13 *Barnes Common (London)* The Standard in Cornhill, for example one in Godstone dated 1744, another at Claremont Park, Esher dated 1747, and a third in Upper Richmond Road, East Sheen (London) dated 1751. The stone in Lewes High Street (Sussex) also gives the distance to The Standard.

Several other London landmarks were also used as measuring points. Milestones along the A3 going north from Clapham Common give mileages to the Royal Exchange and Whitehall, while the obelisk at Southwark shows Palace Yard in Westminster and Fleet Street (**37**). The traditional starting point for roads to East Anglia was Whitechapel. An obelisk in Snaresbrook (London) stands where the roads to Newmarket and Chigwell diverge. Although the inscription is now badly eroded, earlier descriptions record it as 6 miles, 6 furlongs, 24 poles to Stones End, Whitechapel (see Chapter 5 for further details). A stone at Hamels Park, Puckeridge (Herts.) gives 'XXVIII Miles from Shore Ditch Church London'. This was one of the measuring points for the Great North Road. Another ecclesiastical measuring point was Bow Bells, as shown on the rebus posts of East Sussex (27) (see Chapter 4 for more details). The obelisk near Richmond Bridge hedges its bets by showing mileages to Hyde Park Corner, and to Westminster, Blackfriars and London Bridges.

Strangely, no set rules operate for fixing datum points for measuring modern roads, and only a local Highways Department can give an idea of what is used in that particular area. Roads from many larger towns often take their measurements from an inner ring road where car parks are usually sited and visitors would normally end their road journeys, as endeavours are made to keep traffic out of town centres.

For villages the church often acts as the measuring point if it is situated fairly near the centre. Village greens may also be used, or some other central feature. These datum points, however, are by no means standard, and a point may be taken whose historical precedent has long been forgotten. It is not uncommon, still, in rural areas to find a finger post giving a certain distance to a village, while a mile further on another finger post gives exactly the same mileage. The explanation is that the road was originally measured from different points and the distances have never been up-dated.

Most capital cities have a point from which the principal national routes are measured. Today mileages from London are calculated from the site of the original Queen Eleanor's Cross which is now occupied by an equestrian statue of Charles I at the edge of Trafalgar Square. A metal plate set in the pavement just behind the plinth records this fact (14). In Paris a bronze plaque shaped like a compass rose is set in the pavement in front of Notre Dame cathedral and states that it is Kilometre Zero of all

47

the roads of France. Spain has a similar marker, a semi-circular stone set in the pavement in the Puerta del Sol in Madrid and showing a map of the country. Kilometre Zero in Buenos Aires is a stone pillar in the Plaza del Congresso with a map of Argentina and the main roads radiating from the capital carved on it, with a dedication to the Virgin of Lujan, patron saint of roads.

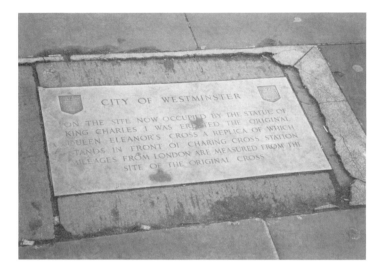

14 *Trafalgar Square (London)*

Maps

Clay tablets showing maps survive from Babylonian times, and Roman travellers often carried pottery plaques listing the road stations on their route and the distances between them. The best record of routes and distances in Roman Britain comes from the Antonine Itinerary, made in the late second or early third century AD. It gives routes all over the Roman empire, listing staging posts and the distances between them, which correspond fairly well with modern distances. It was probably produced for official travellers.

The Peutinger Table was produced in about the third century AD but only a thirteenth-century copy remains. It is a sketch map of the Roman empire showing roads and towns, with symbols to represent such amenities as posting stations and baths. Although in parts it is very inaccurate, a Roman milestone found near Afula, Israel, in 1973 corresponds to the distance in the Peutinger Table. It shows thirty-four miles, which matches the mileage to Caesarea on the coast. The edges of the map have been damaged, and little of Britain, on the fringe of the empire, remains. The map was found in Worms and was given to Conrad Peutinger of Augsburg in 1508. It is now kept in Vienna.

Travel in medieval times was probably more widespread than we realise, mainly relying on experience together with advice and rudimentary maps passed on by other travellers and local people along the way. There is documentary evidence to show that those who could afford it hired guides to lead them over difficult moorland, across fens, or to the easiest ford. Maps showing roads in Britain have survived from the thirteenth century, while the first road books - maps showing specific main routes with the towns passed through and distances between them and with written commentaries - appeared in the mid-sixteenth century.

In 1533 Henry VIII gave permission to a young scholar called John Leland to search the libraries of monasteries for works by ancient writers before they were lost in the dissolution. Leland spent six years travelling the country in search of material, and in 1541 published his *Itinerary*, the first road book of Britain.

John Ogilby (1600-1676), cosmographer and geographic printer to Charles II, published his *Britannia* in 1675. It was the first accurately surveyed road book of England and Wales, and the first to use the statute mile. In strip maps it showed about 7,500 miles of main routes between cities, together with such features as rivers and woods, mills, bridges, gallows and local industries. His maps are peppered with such useful comments as 'Great corn fields on both sides' or 'extraordinary durty lane'. Hills are drawn in as small mounds, the summit uppermost if the traveller ascends them, but upside down to show a descent. Enclosed roads have a solid outline, while those across open land have a broken line, just as on present-day Ordnance Survey maps. Place names were spelt phonetically, probably reflecting how the surveyor heard them spoken - Namptwich (Nantwich), Dullidge (Dulwich), Belreikey (Billericay), Foy (Fowey), and Shipton Mallard (Shepton Mallett).

Ogilby was the first to survey roads thoroughly. Engravings illustrating *Britannia* show his surveyors with tools of their trade - theodolite and measuring wheel. The roads are shown drawn vertically on long scrolls, several segments to the page and working from bottom left to top right of the page, each scroll having a compass rose to show the direction of travel. It was, however, a large, expensive volume, suitable for a gentleman's library, but not for slipping into the pocket of a traveller. Ogilby's maps were subsequently used by many other printers to produce their own road books. *Britannia Depicta*, published in 1720 by Emanual Bowen, was a half-scale reduction of Ogilby's maps with certain improvements which attempted to give a pocket edition of the itinerary. It is unlikely that the roads were resurveyed, although some spellings were standardised.

As roads improved, more people journeyed round England for business and for pleasure. There was therefore an increasing demand for road maps. Those with time and money to spare wrote about their travels, some for publication, others for private enjoyment. It is probable that Daniel Defoe made much use of Camden's *Britannia* published in 1695 during his travels around Britain. A volume of it was catalogued in his library after his death. At the end of the eighteenth century, the Hon. John Byng wrote that he was 'tolerably well accompany'd with touring, road books, maps etc. ... The many maps I shall have with me are very antient, and before the baneful luxury of turnpikes was public ...' He travelled for pleasure each summer, usually on horseback but sometimes in a chaise, and could cover six hundred miles in two months. He wanted the accounts of his journeys published, but not for at least one hundred years after his death because he considered that too many such books were being produced. When Robert Southey wanted to write a travel book, he decided it would carry more appeal if it purported to come from the pen of a foreign visitor to this country. He therefore used the pseudonym of Don Manuel Alvarez Espriella. He mentions purchasing in Exeter 'a map of England folded for the pocket, with the roads and distances all marked upon it. I purchased also a book of the roads, in which not only the distance of every place in the kingdom from London, and from each other, is set down, but also the best inn at each place is pointed out, the name mentioned of every gentleman's seat near the road, and the objects which are most worthy a traveller's notice.'

Until the mid-eighteenth century, most maps had recorded only places adjacent to main highways, waterways or the coast. It was becoming increasingly obvious that accurately surveyed maps of the entire country were needed, not just for travellers, but also for military purposes. The Rev. William Borlase, Vicar of Ludgvan near Penzance, wrote to his friend Henry Baker suggesting that the newly-formed Society of Arts, of which Baker was a founder member, should offer rewards for producing county maps.[9] After much discussion, the Society, in 1759, offered a premium of £100 to anyone making an accurate survey of a particular county, 'the Horizontal Distances of all places in the Map to be taken with the Theodolite or Plane Table and the roads to be measured with a Perambulator and noted down in Figures'. This was probably spelt out because surveyors were conservative, and although more accurate and improved instruments were available, they tended to employ versions that had been in use since Elizabethan times. The scale had to be standardised at one inch to one mile, and the maps were to be produced in two years. It was hoped that the individual county maps would eventually provide a complete survey of England.

In the first seven years, only two awards were made, to Benjamin Donn for a map of Devon and to Peter Burdett for a map of Derbyshire. Both had taken longer than two years to produce their maps because of the difficulty of covering the ground in the winter or in bad weather, and because of delays in engraving and printing. Between 1767 and 1786 awards were made for maps of Northumberland, Leicestershire, Somerset and Suffolk, and from 1787 to 1801 when the prizes ceased, for maps of Hampshire, Sussex, Lancashire and Oxfordshire.

The maps were carefully assessed and checked by referees but many failed to meet the Society's high standards. Other professional cartographers, notably William Faden, bought the engraved plates of maps that had not made the grade, and published revised editions to fill the gaps where county maps did not exist. By the beginning of the nineteenth century, therefore, almost every county had a topographical map of at least one inch to one mile, but the standards and accuracy differed too much to bring them all together into a uniform map of the whole country.

It was not only the Society of Arts that had been working towards an accurate map of Britain. After the Jacobite uprising of 1745, a thorough survey of Scotland was undertaken by Lt William Roy. He first suggested extending the survey to the whole country in 1763, and after his appointment as Inspector-General of Coasts under the Board of Ordnance two years later, all his work was undertaken with this end in mind.[10]

In 1782 the Duke of Richmond became Master-General of the Board of Ordnance which was responsible for fortifications and the defence of the kingdom. The Duke owned large estates in West Sussex, including Goodwood, and was almost unique in employing professional surveyors for his properties. His surveyors, Thomas Yeakell and William Gardner, also did private work, and were later employed by the Board of Ordnance which adopted many of their techniques.

William Roy, by then a Major General, died in 1790, but the Duke of Richmond continued Roy's project and in June 1791 the trigonometrical survey of England began. The success of the undertaking was made possible by a very accurate three foot altazimuth theodolite which had been made by Jesse Ramsden in 1784 and paid for by King George IV. The Duke of Richmond acquired a second instrument which had been made for the East India Company for a survey in India, but which was not delivered due to a business disagreement. Because of the threat of possible invasion by the French, the survey concentrated first on the counties in the south-east, and maps of Kent were published in 1801. The surveyors used a scale of two inches to one mile in order to show such features as field boundaries. The maps were reduced to one inch to one mile for engraving from the surveyors' drawings. Between 1841 and 1888 six inch to one mile maps of Britain were produced, and these are invaluable because of the outstanding amount of detail shown on them.

Until the mid-1970s the post of Director General of the Ordnance Survey was always held by a senior army officer. Surveying techniques have changed dramatically since the world's only national mapping organisation was founded over two hundred years ago. Measurements by simple theodolites eventually gave way to aerial and then satellite photography. The advent of the computer enabled mapping data to be stored in digital form and computational processing of this information now allows maps to be produced for a great variety of purposes.

Since the county councils were first set up in 1888, and particularly in the latter half of the twentieth century, the constantly changing administrative divisions of Britain have caused growing confusion over the identity of counties. Areas were redrawn with more regular shapes; a protruberance was carved off and given to the county it jutted into; a small county was amalgamated with a larger neighbour. The county of Middlesex was absorbed by Greater London for administrative purposes in 1965, but the historic county still exists and the name is used in postal addresses. Although swallowed up by Leicestershire for its local government, Rutland proudly proclaims its geographical presence with road signs. New counties called Avon, Cleveland and Humberside were created only to be abolished in 1996. Modern mapmakers use these administrative boundaries, and while the historic divisions can be just as perplexing, with some cities such as Exeter, Bristol,

Lichfield and Newcastle-upon-Tyne being counties in their own right, the borders had remained fairly constant for centuries. For simplicity, the boundaries used on modern Ordnance Survey maps have been used in this book.[11]

CHAPTER 4

Milestones in England:
From Roman Roads to Turnpikes

Roman Milestones

The first genuine milestones to be set up as marks of measured distance were put in place by the Romans, who enjoyed travelling for business or amusement, apart from military reasons, and regarded mobility as a boost to social standing. Over 4,000 milestones with inscriptions have been found throughout the former Roman Empire, in modern countries such as Israel, Spain, Switzerland, Egypt, France and Tunisia. They were mostly cylindrical or oval-plan columns up to four metres high, often set in a square base. The earliest to have been found dates from 252 BC. Many of them have lengthy inscriptions, and one found at Sirmium (now Mitrovica northwest of Belgrade), after giving a long list of the titles of the reigning Emperor Caesar Flavius Julius Constantius, goes on to state that 'after having built the roads, remade the bridges, restored the common prosperity, he has set up across Illyria milestones every 5 miles from the river Atras to the River Sava 364 miles'. Other stones give details of who paid for the building of the road, or give information about bridges, causeways or flood prevention works. A stone from Egypt tells the traveller that the Emperor Hadrian built the road 'with copious cisterns, resting stations and garrisons at intervals along the road', while another found in former Yugoslavia records that the road was cut through the mountains thus eliminating the curves. A stone dating from AD 69 found in Israel indicates that the road was built by a legion.

In some cases milestones were re-cut, especially when a new Emperor came to power. The stone might be turned round and the new inscription put on the reverse, or it could be inverted and reworked. Other milestones were merely discarded and replaced, the old stone being either left near its original site, or, more often, taken away to be used as building material.

The Romans built over 8,000 miles of roads in Britain. It is unlikely that they put stones at every mile on every road; had they done so, many thousands of milestones should have been found, whereas only about 110 have been discovered. A few of these stones bear no inscription at all and it is only their shape and location which signifies their probable purpose. Most, however, are inscribed with the name of an emperor, but not always with a mileage. In lowland areas it is possible that wooden markers were used which have not survived the passage of time, while in regions with abundant natural stone, rough, uncut blocks with painted lettering may have served the same purpose. Stones with incised characters usually had the lettering picked out in red paint.

Of the stones that do bear inscriptions, most just give the name and titles of the reigning emperor, reminding the populace of his god-like status. The inscriptions are in very abbreviated form which need an experienced Roman historian to decipher. Only examples found in England have been given; Roman milestones have, however, also been found in Wales and Scotland.

A milestone found a mile south of Caster (Cambs.) reads 'IMP.CAS / M.ANNIO / FLORIANO / P.F.INVICTO./ AVG / M.P.I.' or 'Imp(eratori) Caes(ari)/M(arco) Annio/Floriano/P(io) F(elici) Invicto/Aug(usto)/m(ille) p(assus) I' which is translated as 'For the Emperor Caesar Marcus Annius Florianus Pius Invictus Augustus, one mile'.[1] The emperor's name serves to date the stone fairly accurately. Florian reigned in AD 276. Another stone which gives a mileage was dug up in a garden in Buxton (Derbys.) - the Roman spa town of Aquae Arnemetiae - in 1862. Only a partial inscription remains, the translation of which is '... with tribunician power, twice consul, father of his country, from Navio 11 miles'.[2]   Brough-on-Noe was the Roman fort of Navio, and a road ran from Buxton through Brough to Sheffield.

An imposing cylindrical milestone nearly 8 ft (2.4 m) high was found in the bed of a stream near Caton, four miles from Lancaster, in 1803.   It commemorates the Emperor Hadrian (AD 119-138), and the inscription ends with the distance '4 miles', no doubt denoting the mileage from Lancaster along a branch road to the fort at Overborrow.[3]

In 1885 seven milestones were found at Crindledykes Farm, one mile from the Roman fort of Vindolanda (Northumb.). The only one to show a mileage has the following lengthy text: 'For the Emperor Caesar Marcus Aurelius Severus Alexander Pius Felix Augustus, pontifex maximus, in his second year of tribunician power, consul, father of his country, under the charge of Claudius Xenophon, emperor's propraetorian legate, 14 miles'.[4] The distance is to Corbridge along the road called Stanegate, which runs to the south of Hadrian's Wall. Another milestone dedicated to the Emperor Severus Alexander (AD 222-223) and also erected under the governorship of Claudius Xenophon was found three years earlier near milecastle 42 at Cawfields.[4] It records a distance of 18 miles, probably measured from Portgate, where the Military Way, a service road running just behind Hadrian's Wall, joins Dere Street which runs from York to Edinburgh. At Henshaw near Vindolanda (Northumb.), a cylindrical milestone still stands in its original position beside the Stanegate, but no inscription is visible on it. Some other Roman milestones still *in situ* can be found at Kirkby Thore and Middleton (Cumbria), and at Birtley and Chesterholm (Northumb.).   All are scheduled Ancient Monuments in the care of English Heritage. In the south of England, a probable Roman milestone found at Stinsford (Dorset) was repositioned on a roundabout in 1988 to mark the opening of the Dorchester bypass.

Evidence of local involvement in road construction comes from a milestone found in Lincoln (see also Chapter 6), which reads 'For the Emperor Caesar Publius Licinius

Valerianus Pius Felix Augustus, pontifex maximus, with tribunician power, father of his country, the municipality of Lindum set this up.'[5] This dates from the reign of Valerian from AD 253-259. Another stone, which has now been lost, read 'For the Emperor Caesar Marcus Antonius Gordianus Pius Felix Augustus, the canton of the Belgae set this up'. It was reputedly found in the Roman town wall at Bitterne (Clausentum) near Southampton (Hants). The capital of the tribal area of the Belgae was at Winchester. The Emperor Gordian III reigned from AD 238-244.

Another region, that of the Dobunni, whose capital was at Cirencester, set up a stone, a fragment of which was found in a wall at Kenchester (Magnis) (Her. & Worcs.). It reads 'IMP/MAR.AUR/NUMORIAN/O/RPDC...' (For the Emperor Caesar Marcus Aurelius Numerianus the canton of the Dobunni set this up).[6] Numerian was emperor from AD 283-284.

Examples of stones that were recut include an imposing cylindrical milestone, nearly 6 ft (1.8 m) high and showing the distance to York, which was first dedicated to the Emperor Decius (AD 250-251). It was then inverted and a new inscription cut, partly overlapping the first: 'For the Emperor-Caesars Vibius Gallus and Gaius Veldumnianus Volusianus, Pius Felix Augustus: from Eboracum 22 miles'. Gallus and Volusian reigned from AD 251-253. The stone was found at Castleford (Yorks.) in about 1880 during work on a public drain. It was set up in the garden of the Town Surveyor, but in 1897 was purchased for Leeds Museum.[7]

A milestone found in the river Petterill just south of Carlisle in 1894 seems to have had three separate inscriptions. The first was probably in the centre of the 6 ft 2 in (1.8 m) pillar, but was chiselled away before the message 'For the Emperor Caesar Marcus Aurelius Mausaeus Carausius Pius Felix Invictus Augustus' was cut at the top (Carausius, AD 286-293). The stone was later inverted and 'For Flavius Valerius Constantinus, most noble Caesar' (Constantine I, AD 306-307) was put at the other end.[8]

In 1924 two milestones were found in a ditch beside the Roman road across Stainmore (Yorks.).[9] One has an inscription to Florian (AD 276) almost obliterated by a dedication to Probus (AD 276-282). The second stone commemorates Carus (AD 282-230) and it is quite possible that the first stone, having been used twice, was discarded and a new one put in its place. In an area of abundant natural stone, they were not re-used in buildings but lay abandoned close to their original positions.

Another of the milestones found at Crindledykes Farm has had four texts chiselled over each other, sometimes incorporating part of one of the earlier ones. The emperors commemorated are Constantius (AD 296-305), Constantinus I (AD 306-307), Maximianus (AD 305-311) and Maximinus Daia (AD 309-313).[4] Constantine the Great (AD 307-337) is mentioned on a milestone found at Caves Inn, Shawell (Leics.) in 1963. It is of an unusual squared, tapering shape and was found, broken into three pieces, in a well.[10] It is made of sandstone, probably from a quarry at Duston eighteen miles away.

These are just a few examples of the Roman milestones that have been found in England. One of the most complete lists of them is in Jeffrey Sedgeley's survey of the stone utilised by the Romans and the quarries from which it came (see Bibliography). He concluded that most Roman milestones were quarried within a few miles of the site where they were to be used. His report also gives the present locations of these milestones, and although most are in museums, they are unfortunately not always on display. An account of some of the uses to which redundant Roman milestones were put can be found in Chapter 6.

Small Wayside Milestones

After the collapse of Roman control in Britain early in the fifth century, twelve hundred years elapsed before milestones reappeared beside our roads. The term 'small wayside milestone' has been given to those erected from the seventeenth century onwards and usually found on roadside verges or pavements, and frequently overlooked because they are hidden in vegetation or lost in the brick and concrete of a townscape. They are often part of a series put up by a turnpike trust, local parishes, district or county councils, or sometimes privately. They have been divided according to what they are made of - stone, stone and cast iron, cast iron - and these divisions also roughly correspond to the development of the different styles. Small wayside stones constitute the majority of milestones in England and are in the greatest danger of being damaged by verge cutting machines, disappearing during road works, or of being abandoned when broken in traffic accidents. There is a great diversity of shapes and styles. Most are difficult to date, but some do conveniently show the year of their manufacture, and even who made them, and if documentary evidence exists, information can be found about their origins. In the days before instant mass communication, new ideas spread slowly, and developments occurred at different periods in different areas, making it difficult to put each style into a definite time bracket. Some turnpike trusts may have resisted innovations in style, while others could not afford new stones and merely had the worn ones repaired. The lower cost of local raw materials must also have affected choice of style. However there are clues to look for that can place most milestones in an approximate period.

Stone
It is probable that the first mileposts, put up in the late seventeenth and early eighteenth centuries, were made of wood, but none have survived. The earliest surviving post-Roman milestones date from the early eighteenth century. They are made of stone, a square pillar or a 'tombstone' shape being the most popular. A few square stone pillars had inscriptions on all four sides and were almost certainly originally sited at cross-roads, although they have now been repositioned because of road alterations. However, most early milestones usually have the inscription on the face parallel to the road and use Roman numerals, and although it is impossible to say that these features

60

always signify an early to mid-eighteenth-century stone, they can often be a good guide as to its age. Other indicators are the use of the upright s (f), and the use of an obsolete name or spelling of a town, such as Brighthelmstone (Brighton), Sarum (Salisbury), Gloster (Gloucester), or Winton (Winchester).

A correspondent to the *Reading Mercury* in May 1767, commenting on a journey he had taken along the Bath road, suggested that '... if the numbers on them [milestones] were to be in Arabic figures, instead of the Roman letters, they would be more easily read by the passengers, as the post-chaises pass by them very fast: thus for instance, 49 is more easily read than XLVIIII'.[11] From about this time there was a gradual change from Roman to Arabic numerals when new stones were made, and sometimes a replacement by Arabic numerals when worn stones were recut.

It was also realised that an inscription parallel to the road could only be read when the traveller was abreast of it, so stones then had their side faces inscribed or were set corner-wise to the road, giving faces that could be read as one approached. Triangular or wedge shapes then came into use, and the addition of a flattened 'spine' or a raised upper face gave extra surfaces for inscriptions, allowing more information to be given without the need for a pillar of monumental proportions.

Some stones have a corrugated appearance, which was caused by the cutting technique. A line of holes was drilled into a large slab of stone and wedges were driven in until the two pieces of stone split apart. Over the years the ridges have weathered and often worn away, but in sheltered places the corrugations are still clearly visible. In some instances it has been possible to trace the stone to a particular quarry, and a lot more work could be done on this subject. Like icebergs, a considerable length of the milestone was usually hidden below the surface, enabling the post to remain firm and upright. The part meant to be buried was generally left rough-hewn. Traditionally milestones were painted white with black lettering and entries can be found in turnpike trust minutes ordering the road surveyor to see that the painting was done. Travellers would certainly have had difficulty seeing the milestones had they not been painted. There is evidence that certain types of stone were chosen by some turnpike trusts because they took paint well. Nowadays highway authorities do not always have the resources to continue painting and repairing milestones. It is also thought that paint damages the stone by not allowing it to 'breathe', and in some areas milestones are now deliberately being left unpainted, although one wonders whether this is just a convenient excuse for saving money. The letters were often plugged with lead to prevent weathering, and sometimes traces of the metal can still be seen in the incised characters.

Possibly the earliest dated milestone in England stands in the High Street in Beckenham (London) (**10**). Being at a road junction, the square stone pillar has inscriptions on three sides, and it certainly needs the space for the very detailed directions. Croydon Market Place is indicated as IV miles 6 furlongs through the town, Bromley Market Place 1 mile 5 furlongs by the left hand road, and The Swan in Wickham 2 miles 4 furlongs by the right hand road. The stone was erected by the Parish Surveyor in 1713, and in recent years has been moved from a position outside the churchyard to the opposite corner of the road. The oldest surviving set of milestones, and certainly the most documented, is the Trinity Hall series on the old coach road from Cambridge towards London (**15**). Dr William Mouse, or Mowse, a Master of Trinity Hall who died in 1586, left the residue of his estate (about £1,000) to his executor, Robert Hare, for charitable purposes. Hare added about £600 of his own, and with this sum he purchased the manor of Wallpool, the annual rent from which was to be used by the college for the repair of some of the roads around Cambridge, and particularly the old London road from Cambridge as far as Barkway. In 1725, Dr William Warren, a Fellow of Trinity Hall and trustee to the charity, began surveying the road to Barkway and over the next three years he set up sixteen milestones. The fifth, tenth and fifteenth stones were larger than the others and had the arms of Trinity Hall carved on them. His measurements were taken from a mark on the south west buttress of Great St

Mary's church in Cambridge, now commemorated by a circular plaque (see also Chapter 3). Between 1728 and 1732 Dr Warren replaced the first set of stones, except for the fifth, tenth and fifteenth which had been made in 1725, 1726 and 1727 respectively, with a new set, each larger than its predecessor and made of Portland stone, and each bearing the arms of Trinity Hall at the top and the date in Roman numerals at the base. Most of the stones can still be found, mainly along the B1368. Their condition varies, and some are set more deeply in the ground, thus obliterating the lower inscriptions.

15 *Fowlmere (Cambs.)*   **16** *Blickling (Norfolk)*

The one-mile stone at Trumpington now stands at a busy junction on the Cambridge ring road. It was erected on 25 April 1728 to commemorate the visit of King George II to the university. At the top it bears the arms of Dr Mouse impaled with the crescent of Trinity Hall and cost £5 8s. 0d. (£5.40). In his account of how he set up the milestones, Dr Warren wrote: 'On ye First stone these words in Capitals "I Mile to Great Saint

Maries Church Cambridge A.D. MDCCXXVIII'".[12]   Changes were made to the inscription in later years. An etching of 1838 shows this stone depicting 'I/MILE TO/GREAT SAINT/ MARIES CHURCH/CAMBRIDGE/☞/AD/ MDCCXXVII/Lt St Maries'. Another drawing by Charles Harper published in 1902 shows the date as 1727 in Arabic numerals,[13] while a sketch in a guide book of 1965 has the latter date in Roman numerals once again, but the 'Lt St Maries' has disappeared below the pavement. It is probable that over the years the inscription wore away and was recut several times, on one occasion losing a 'I' from the end of the date. Now, sadly, the date has gone too, and the pavement level has risen to just below the pointing hand.

The 2-, 3-, and 4-mile stones date from 1729, the 6-, 7-, 8- and 9-mile from 1730, the 11- and 12-mile from 1731, and the 13- and 14-mile from 1732. All have the crescent arms of Trinity Hall carved at the top of the pillar. Below is the distance to Cambridge in Roman numerals, a black-painted pointing hand, and beneath that the date, also in Roman numerals.

At the junction of the B1368 and the A505, the 11-mile stone is lozenge-shaped, possibly to reflect the shape of the cross-roads. The 16-mile stone in Barkway (Herts.) was set up on 29 May 1728 on the anniversary of King Charles II's birth and restoration. It has the arms of Robert Hare and of Trinity Hall carved at the top. When Dr Warren first placed the stone in Barkway it stood outside The Angel. By the beginning of this century the inn had become The Wheat Sheaf. The fairly new building against which it stands today has been named Milestone House. The 15-mile stone is no longer the original, and this, along with the 13-, 14- and 16-mile stones (all in Hertfordshire) has a cast iron plate which covers most of the original inscription and gives distances to London, Barkway and Cambridge. The plates probably date from the early nineteenth century and were placed there by the Wadesmill Turnpike Trust which by then was responsible for the road through Barkway as far as the county boundary at Barley.

Not content with measuring the London road, Dr Warren then set to work again with his chain and in May 1731 started measuring the road towards Haverhill (Suffolk). Over the next nine years ten milestones were set up along the road, and the first can be found at the junction of Station Road and Hill Road in Cambridge, erected, according to Dr Warren's diary, in memory of a Mr Worts who had left money in his will for mending the road to the Gogmagog Hills. In 1735 he turned his attention to the Cambridge to Huntingdon road and the first five miles were marked with stones. Only the stones along the London road, however, bear the Trinity Hall arms.

There are many other examples of simple, square stone pillars with the mileage on the face parallel to the road, and also showing other characteristics of an early to mid-eighteenth-century milestone. Some give just one destination, and if the road was one of the early turnpikes, the stone probably predates the General Turnpike Act of 1767 which required the towns at either end of the road to be shown. The road from Ashbourne to Buxton (Derbys.) was turnpiked in 1738. A milestone near the Ashbourne end of the Tissington Trail reads 'FROM/LONDON/CXL' in crudely-cut lettering. The stone came from the slate quarries at Swithland in Charnwood Forest.

A privately-erected milestone showing several characteristics of an eighteenth-century stone stands on the B1354 in Norfolk and reads 'I/Mile from/Blickling Hou*f*e/ X/Miles from/Holt'. It was probably erected by the Earl of Buckinghamshire of Blickling Hall to guide visitors to his country estate **(16)**.

Some of the best examples of the early square stone pillars can be found on the outskirts of London. They often have inscriptions on three or four of their sides, with two destinations repeated on opposite faces. From dates inscribed on some of them, it seems that the original single inscription was joined at a later date by inscriptions on the sides. Two milestones on Upper Richmond Road in East Sheen and Roehampton give distances to The Standard in Cornhill and to Hyde Park Corner in Roman numerals, and one of the stones is

65

dated 1751. Two similar stones, one dated 1744, the other 1747, at Godstone and Esher (Surrey) respectively, have been described in Chapter 3. A similar one in Sutton High Street (London) is dated 1745. Another series of stones, dated 1744, can be seen along the A40 between High Wycombe and Stokenchurch (Bucks.) with a well-preserved example at Dashwood's Hill. The inscription on the face parallel to the road is in Roman numerals, while the same distance in Arabic numerals is given on the side, almost certainly cut at a later date. The Wycombe to Stokenchurch Turnpike was created in 1719. The well-preserved square stone pillar outside Putney Hospital probably once stood at a cross-roads on Barnes Common. The inscription - 'V/MILES/FROM/HYDE-PARK-CORNER' - is repeated on all four sides (13).

The Stevenage to Biggleswade Turnpike Trust (Herts.) was set up in 1720, and some of its milestones can be found along the old route of the Great North Road. They show the mileages from London in roughly-cut lettering with Arabic numerals. On some of the stones the older Roman numerals can still just be made out. There are several examples of early milestones being recut. Those on the road between Amersham and Tatling End (Bucks.) were turned round and the lettering redone in Arabic numerals. In the process they seem to have become slightly confused as the 23-mile stone has XXIV on the back, the 24-mile XXIII, and the 25-mile XXVI.

On some roads the milestones, although probably still the original square pillars, seem to have been renovated at different times, and now show most of the variations possible in the position of the inscriptions, all now with Arabic numerals. On the B1198 (Cambs.) the stone at Bassingbourn cum Kneesworth has the inscription only on the face parallel to the road: 'B & K/ROYSTON/2/LONDON/40'. Ten miles to the north at Caxton, the front face gives the distance to London, while mileages to Royston and Huntingdon are on either side. A road with even more variation in its square-pillared milestones is the A4129 in Buckinghamshire between the Oxfordshire border near Thame and Princes Risborough. At Aston Sandford the inscriptions are on the faces at right-angles to the road. Two milestones stand in the parish of Longwick, one cornerwise to the road with the mileages on adjacent faces, the second with the mileage on the face parallel to the road. The square stone pillars to be found along the B1040 (Cambs.) have inscriptions on three faces and give the mileage between St Ives and Potton (Beds.) along with the name of the parish. The final stone in the series stands in the centre of Potton and is now in poor condition, but along with the obelisk at Ampthill (see Chapter 6 for full details) they are the only milestones that have survived in Bedfordshire, according to a survey of industrial archaeology in the county. The Potton milestone was found during building work in the 1960s, having probably been buried during World War II.

Many of the local stonemasons who made the milestones also made gravestones, and it was therefore hardly surprising that this shape was used (**11,17,53,59**). Several tombstone-shaped milestones conveniently have a date inscribed on them which gives a guide to when this design was in use. Wiltshire has some excellent examples. One at Mere Down reads 'XXI/MILES FROM/SARUM/XCIX/FROM/LONDON/1750', showing three features of a mid-eighteenth-century stone - inscription parallel to the road, Roman numerals, and the use of the name Sarum for Salisbury. The stone, one of several survivors of this series, stands beside an abandoned coach road which is now a track. On another former coach road between Chitterne and Yarnbury Castle (Wilts.) the milestones are dated 1754. At Amesbury (Wilts.) a fine milestone dated 1764 gives distances in Roman numerals from London and Andover, while on the Warminster to Shaftesbury road, a series dated 1766 shows distances from Shaston (Shaftesbury). Near Badbury (Oxon) a stone reads LXXI Miles from London. A large milestone in the same county, at Headington, denotes Oxford, one mile distant, in capital letters with London, 53 miles away, shown in less significant lower case lettering.

On the road between Hexham and Rothbury (Northumb.) most of the milestones are shaped like one-eighth

67

of a sphere, but beside some of this series can be found earlier tombstone-shaped stones. At Colwell, the older stone reads 'From/Alnwick/XXXV', with the same inscription being just decipherable on the reverse (17). At Little Swinburn, the reverse of the stone reads 'From/Alnwick/XXXIII', while the inscription on the front is in more modern sans serif capitals, into which an unfortunate error has crept (see Chapter 6). The road from Hexham to Alnmouth, known as the Corn Road, was constructed in the 1750s to enable landowners in the area to get their grain to the coast for export.

17 Colwell (Northumb.)

The development of these earliest milestones to Arabic numerals and angled faces seems to have come in a rather haphazard fashion, and some stones show a mixture of styles. At Alberbury (Wilts.) is a stone that reads '4 Miles/to Sarum/XX to/Southton' (Southampton). The turnpike was created in 1753.

A fine, early example of a milestone with Arabic numerals, but with the inscription parallel to the road, is now in Newarke House Museum in Leicester. It was one of a series made for the Market Harborough to Loughborough Turnpike in 1746 by Harry Hind of Swithland slate quarry in Charnwood Forest, at a cost of 15s. (75p) each. This particular stone originally stood in Belgrave Gate, Leicester, and was taller than the others in the series. The number one has been shaped like a capital J. Another stone, obviously made by the same mason with the same unusually shaped figure one has survived *in situ* in Wood Street, Ashby-de-la-Zouch (Leics.). It marks the start of the Ashby to Leicester Turnpike, created in 1753. Between Chilton and Arlington (Berks.) a series of gravestone-shaped milestones with gabled tops and using Arabic numerals stands beside the A34. They are dated 1776.

East of Leicester along the A47 five stones remain of a series giving the mileage to Leicester and Uppingham. They are unusual because the lettering has been chipped into the slightly convex face. Narrower gravestone-shaped milestones can be found along the A352 between Dorchester and Sherborne (Dorset). Most have the name Dorchester arched at the top and Sherborne written horizontally, but one stone near Minterne Magna has both town names arched. They mark part of the routes of the Shaftesbury to Sherborne Turnpike (1752-1877) and the Cerne Abbas Turnpike (1778-1874).

With so many dated examples, it is clear that these two shapes were the earliest fashion in milestone design.

Stones of a triangular plan would have needed less stone to produce than square pillars, and having the faces at an angle to the road enabled travellers to read the inscription as they approached. A good series with distances in Roman numerals stands along the A30 in Wiltshire between Salisbury and Shaftesbury, inscribed as Sarum and Shaston respectively. They are thought to date from about 1800. The sandstone post to the west of Nottingham near the university is eroded and the right hand side is difficult to decipher. The other face reads 'From DERBY/XIII/Miles'. A triangular plan stone has a place in a reconstructed street scene in Newarke House Museum, Leicester. It was found in a ditch near the Market Harborough to Desborough road, probably having been hidden there during World War II. Its inscription, showing Arabic numerals, is now rather worn. Against the wall of Milestone House, now a small general store, but once an alehouse in Ibstock (Leics.), stands a simple triangular milestone showing Hinckley 10 Notts 23. It was defaced during the war, but was renovated a few years ago by being covered with a skin of concrete and having the towns and distances painted on. An example from Northumberland can be found near the present memorial to the Battle of Otterburn. The painted stone with attractive seriffed lettering reads 'Newcastle/31/Miles; Jedbro/25/Miles'. When the Otterburn to Redesdale Turnpike was created in 1777 the stone commemorating the battle, fought in 1388, had to be re-sited. The present milestone is one of a series along the A68 and A696.

Wedge shaped stones - those with the side faces forming a more acute angle (**18**) - were even more economical and are found particularly in Norfolk, a county with no suitable deposits of stone. An almost complete series can be seen along the

18 *Grangemill (Derbys.)*   **19** *Beckhampton (Wilts.)*

twenty miles of the Norwich to Watton road which operated as a turnpike from 1770 to 1870.

Cylindrical stones are not frequently encountered, but some can be found in Oxfordshire. On the A40 towards Oxford a few with Roman numerals can still be seen. The one most easily noticed, near Bury Knowle Park, Headington, reads 'LII/Miles From/London/II/Miles to/Oxford'. At Dorchester-on-Thames a cylindrical stone gives distances to London, Henley, Abingdon and Oxford. It was made for the Henley and Dorchester Turnpike which was created in 1736. Earlier Roman numerals can just be made out beneath the present inscription.

More elaborate, multi-faceted milestones would have been more expensive to produce and are usually a sign of a well-used, affluent turnpike. They are also more likely to have been made in the eighteenth century before the railways began competing for traffic, thereby reducing toll receipts. The main road from London to Bath was one of the busiest routes in the country but was under the control of a number of turnpike trusts, mostly created in the first half of the eighteenth century. Many of its milestones are quite elaborate and a journey today along the A4 will provide a good exercise in locating the sections of road covered by the different turnpike trusts from the shapes of the various series of milestones. On the highway between Maidenhead and Twyford (Berks.) which was turnpiked in 1718 the milestones have a square base and a triangular-plan upper half, one face of which shows the distance to Hyde Park Corner. The lower front face gives the parish name, and sometimes the date 1824 can be seen, but the stones are almost certainly far older and this date probably refers to the year a renovation took place. On the stone at Knowl Hill earlier Roman numerals are still visible on the back. The section from Newbury (Berks.) to Marlborough (Wilts.) became a turnpike in 1726. The milestones in this section may date from 1746 and are of a similar shape to those west of Maidenhead but have the distance to London on the front face. Between Marlborough and Cherhill (Wilts.), turnpiked in 1743, the London mileage is shown on a lozenge-shaped face at the top of the stone. The 82-mile stone near Beckhampton is in good condition (**19**).

Milestones of a similar design can also be found north of Andover (Hants) on the road to Newbury.

Most stone milestones are of a fairly plain and functional appearance. The Trinity Hall series with their coats of arms are possibly unique. Decoration became easier and more popular with the advent of cast iron. However, a few stones can be found with extra embellishments. Carved hands pointing the way are occasionally found, and examples can be seen on a square pillar at Slack (Yorks.) and a gravestone-shaped milestone at Wilpshire (Lancs.). Five very assertive pointing fingers grace a gable-topped stone pillar at Blackshaw Head near Hebden Bridge (Yorks.). The small square pillar one mile west of Long Sutton (Lincs.) has a decorative squiggle beneath the inscription on the side faces. A series of wedge-shaped stones on the turnpike created in 1811

20 *Barnacre (Lancs.)*

between Ashbourne and Haddon (Derbys.) has a very flamboyant 𝕿 in the word 'To' (**18**). Between Preston and Garstang (Lancs.) a series of cylindrical milestones still survives from the Preston to Lancaster road turnpiked in 1751. The sandstone pillars display beautiful script lettering (**20**). Another wedge-shaped stone at Crows an Wra (Cornwall) might almost have been a stonemason's sampler. On one side the distances to Penzance and Land's End are pleasingly set out with the destinations arched over the mileage and hands to point the way. On the other side the hand pointing to St Just is larger and the elaborate lettering of the word 'Miles' with its curls and flourishes makes one feel the mason was having a good day.

72

Stone with metal plates

By the second half of the eighteenth century cast iron was becoming more widely used. In 1709 Abraham Darby succeeded in smelting iron with coke at his blast-furnace in Coalbrookdale, Shropshire. Charcoal had been used for fuel since the fifteenth century, but the wood for making it was in increasingly short supply. Coal for producing coke was abundant locally, and enabled the industry to grow and thrive. It took some years for the techniques to be perfected, but by the end of the eighteenth century, virtually all cast iron came from coke blast-furnaces and the diversity of products increased. Its first appearance on milestones was as a plate fixed to a stone. Often this was done when the inscription on the stone had become too worn to read and needed renewing. A cast iron plate was then placed over the original inscription. The vast majority of these metal mileages are fixed parallel to the road, indicating that they were probably late eighteenth century, or renovations of earlier milestones, although unfortunately this is not a fool-proof method of dating them.

There were several methods of attaching the metal plate to the stone. The simplest was to fill holes drilled into the stone post with wood or lead, then to hammer a wrought iron spike through corresponding holes in the cast iron plate into the plug in the stone. An alternative fastening method was to have a bolt going from the plate right through the stone with a nut at the back. A variation of this technique was to have a loop cast in the centre back of the plate. A bolt with a hook at the end was put through the stone support from back to front and the hook looped into the eye on the plate. A nut was then tightened at the other end of the bolt at the back of the stone to hold the plate in place.

Milestones with metal plates must have been the easiest to dismantle during World War II, and it is probable that many of the cast iron plates were melted down and lost forever. Many stone supports can be found with an indented panel and holes where the metal plate was once attached. In some cases the stone support was lost but the plate survived and has now been fixed to a nearby wall.

Some of the earliest cast iron plates had incised lettering, made to resemble the incised lettering on stone (**50**). The best remaining examples can be found in Gloucestershire, Wiltshire and Somerset. Probably some of the oldest milestones with cast iron plates are on roads to Bath and Bristol. One at Southmead (Glos.) reads 'To/Bri*f*tol/3'. A series can be seen between Wincanton and Ilchester (Somerset). The plates are of an attractive shield shape with curved top and the topmost town name arched to match. On some plates an upright 's' has been used. This design was used by both the Ilminster Turnpike Trust (created in 1759) and by the Wincanton Turnpike Trust (created in 1756). Other plates of the same pattern can be found at West Camel between Ilchester and Castle Cary (Somerset), and between Wincanton (Somerset) and Hindon (Wilts.). The Bruton Turnpike Trust, which functioned from 1756 to 1876, and incorporated a network of roads around Bruton, used a square plate showing the mileage, with 'BRUTON' curved above it. An example can be found near North Brewham (Somerset).

The majority of cast iron plates, however, have raised lettering. Most of these plates on stones are square or rectangular in shape. A series can be seen on the road between Brackley and Buckingham (Bucks.). A few yards from an eighteenth-century tollhouse at Broughton Aluph (Kent) is a plate giving distances to Canterbury and Ashford. At Coldwall Bridge, Thorpe, on the Derbyshire side of the River Dove, is a large gritstone block with a small cast iron plate bolted to it reading simply 'CHEADLE/ll'. It was set up in 1822. The Blythe Marsh to Thorpe Turnpike crossed the river here and is now a picturesque bridleway. A series of square stone pillars with rectangular cast iron plates stands along the road from Corhampton to Bishop's Waltham (Hants) giving the mileage to London and Southton (Southampton). A milestone thought to date from the 1830s is now in Newarke House Museum,

Leicester. The plate reads 'TO/ HINCKLEY/ 12/ TO/ LEICESTER/1'. The stone is Swithland slate.

A fine, large plate is fixed to a tombstone-shaped stone at Bradley Mount three miles north of Macclesfield (Cheshire). Distances are also given to London and Stockport. The rounded heads of the wrought iron spikes used to secure the plate to the stone are very evident at each corner. The maker's name has been cast near the bottom of the plate, but it is now very difficult to read, although the place of business can be made out as Macclesfield. There was not usually very much space on the plates for casting the maker's name or a date, but occasionally these can be found. Hampshire has numerous good examples, although some are modern replicas. Between Alton and Odiham on the B3349 the metal plates were made by W. F. Blake, the one near Shalden being easy to find. Some of the milestones on the road going north from Southampton towards Winchester have had their metal plates replaced (**21**). The road became a turnpike in 1757. On the reverse of the 2-mile stone the date 1786 can be made out, along with what looks like a capital R with its mirror image, possibly a stonemason's mark. During a survey undertaken in the 1960s some of the cast iron plates in this series were recorded as missing. Replicas with the cast mark 'Wessex Casting Techniques 1988' at the base were made for the 1- and 2-mile stones out of Southampton. The 5-mile stone in Chandler's Ford has a different style of lettering and was cast by IRS Ltd of Swaffham (Norfolk). The new plates, however, still give the old names of Winton for Winchester and Southton for Southampton.

Another popular shape was the inverted shield, that is with the plate having a straight base and an arched top. An attractive plate with the lettering arched to match the top stands at Southborough (Kent) on the former Sevenoaks to Tunbridge Wells Turnpike showing 'LONDON/33/TUNBRIDGE/3'. A series in Hertfordshire with similar arched lettering marks the route of the former Wadesmill Turnpike to Royston (present A10) along with its branch from Puckeridge to Barkway (B1368). The present metal plates may have been added early in

75

the nineteenth century. The road between Flimwell (Kent) and Rye (Sussex) became a turnpike in 1762. In recent years any missing cast iron plates on the series of eighteen milestones have been replaced. According to a survey undertaken in the 1970s, the plates on the stones in Kent were painted with black lettering on a white background, while those in Sussex had white lettering on a black background. On the A46 and A433 in Gloucestershire, a series of tombstone-shaped stones with a large square metal plate with curved top gives mileages in Roman numerals to Cirencester, Tetbury and Bath. A milestone on the Gosport road at Farringdon (Hants) was recorded as defaced in the 1960s. It now carries a smart, modern replacement plate.

21 *Southampton (Hants)*　　　　**22** *Buckland Newton (Dorset)*

The conventional shield shape with a horizontal top and curved base is not so common. A fine series stands along the former Norwich, Swaffham and Mattishall Turnpike (Norfolk). This was the third set of milestones made for the road after its creation in 1770. Joseph Stanley, a stone and marble mason of Norwich, was paid £120 11s. 6d. (£120.57) in 1868 for the present milestones, after deducting £7 8s. 6d. (£7.42) for the scrap metal value of the previous cast iron set. The metal plates have been set well into the stone pillars, giving the milestones a much more sophisticated appearance than those made at the turn of the nineteenth century. Twenty-four of the original thirty stones remain, many now by-passed by new sections of the A47. The easiest to see are the two either side of Fransham, that to the west showing 'DEREHAM/6/SWAFFHAM/6'. However, this stone had to be replaced by a concrete post in 1994 after being knocked over and broken. The 5-mile stone to the east of the village is original.

A popular style found in Dorset has a metal plate reminiscent of the shape of the London Underground sign - a rectangle with a semicircle top and bottom. The plates are on white-painted stones, and many of the remaining milestones are now on minor country roads. Examples can be found between Charminster and Buckland Newton (Weymouth, Melcombe Regis and Dorchester Turnpike in operation from 1760 to 1878) (**22**), on the A352 at Winfrith Newburgh (Dorchester and Wool Turnpike, 1768-1876), and between Sherborne and Yetminster on a branch of the Shaftesbury and Sherborne Turnpike (1752-1877). On another part of this turnpike at Yarlington (Somerset) a former inscription showing twenty-six miles to Bath can be seen below the cast iron plate, which probably dates from the late eighteenth century. A plate west of Dorchester reading '2/DORCHESTER/BY THE NEW ROAD/MAIDEN NEWTON/6' dates this stone to 1840 when the Maiden Newton Turnpike Trust altered the route of its road.

Only a few of these metal plaques had extra embellishments. An early plate with incised lettering at Long Cross (Somerset) erected by the Frome Turnpike Trust has arrows pointing to Frome and Wells, and the terminus posts of the Bath Turnpike such as that at Kingsdown (Glos.) have pointing hands.

Although most milestones with cast iron plates have the inscription parallel to the road, a few can be found on stones with two or more faces (**23**). Outside the Red Lion Hotel in Atherstone (Warwicks.) is a triangular stone with metal plates on its side and upper faces. It was known as the '3L' stone because it stated that London, Lincoln and Liverpool were each

23 *Forton (Lancs.)*

24 *Ilminster (Somerset)*

one hundred miles from that spot. In fact London and Liverpool are more than one hundred miles away, while Lincoln is considerably less. One metal plate still shows one hundred miles to London, but the plates on the side faces have been substituted by two closer 'L's - Lutterworth and Litchfield [sic]. The road between Worksop and Mansfield (Notts.) did not become a turnpike until 1822. It has another example of a milestone with metal plates on more than one face, one mile from Worksop and twelve from Mansfield, and may be the sole survivor of the original series. Another triangular stone stands on the outskirts of Oxford. It has oval metal plates on the two side faces and is one of a series of milestones on the Abingdon road. The milestones around Ilminster (Somerset) have very small metal plates on each side face in the form of a horizontal strip of metal with a town name cast on it and a small semi-circular tab below the centre showing the mileage **(24)**. Examples can be seen at Stoke-sub-Hamdon and Dinnington.

A square stone post set cornerwise to the road stands between Brampton and Carlisle (Cumbria). It has two inverted shield shaped plates. A series with two square plates lies between Andover (Hants) and Salisbury (Wilts.).

Metal plates on wooden posts are rarely found nowadays. A few survive of a series south of Lyndhurst on the Christchurch road (Hants). The plate in Upper Brailes (Warwicks.) has been cast with a metal cap to protect the top of the wooden post that supports it (**25**).

The milestones of Thomas Telford
Robert Southey gave the civil engineer Thomas Telford the nickname 'Colossus of Roads'. Although most of Telford's road building was undertaken in Scotland, he was responsible for engineering the mail-coach route from London to Holyhead. Better communications were needed between London and Dublin, but in 1808 the Post Office tried in vain to extend their mail-coach service from Shrewsbury to the port of Holyhead. Twenty-four turnpike trusts were involved, seven of them in Wales, and the further they were from London, the worse the upkeep of the roads. In the late eighteenth century Arthur Young, who travelled around Britain commenting mainly on agriculture, had made some very scathing remarks about Welsh turnpikes, describing them as 'mere rocky lanes, full of hugeous stones as big as one's horse, and abominable holes'. A Commission was set up and Telford was appointed to survey the route. Nine commissioners were appointed and £20,000 was granted for the improvements. Work started in 1817 and took fifteen years to complete. The existing turnpike trusts continued to operate and a proportion of the tolls they collected went towards the cost of road improvement, while the Holyhead Road Commissioners supervised the expenditure of the government grants. Royal Mail coaches were exempt from paying tolls.

Telford built his roads using the Roman method of stone foundations, and his roads were made to last. His methods were more expensive than those of Macadam, and for this reason he was not employed by turnpike trusts. His road left London through Barnet, St Albans and Hockliffe, passing through Daventry, Dunchurch, Coventry and Stonebridge, then continuing through Birmingham, Wolverhampton, Shrewsbury, Llangollen, Capel Curig, Bangor and across the Menai Bridge to Holyhead, roughly the route of the Roman Watling Street and the present A5, although new sections of this road have been built in recent years and towns have been by-passed. The major improvements were needed on the Welsh section, and here most of Telford's road is still in use today.

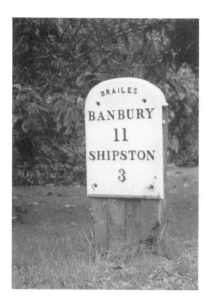 

25 *Upper Brailes (Warwicks.)*   **26** *Blists Hill Museum (Salop)*

Telford was meticulous in his work and he also designed the tollhouses, tollgates and milestones to stand along his road. He wrote that he had spent three years looking all over England for a suitable model for the milestones, but had been unable to find one. His milestones were tall slabs of Anglesey stone with a gabled top. Each one cost £2, and those to be placed at the London end of the road were transported by sea to the Thames. A cast iron plate with pointed top to match the stone was bolted into a recessed panel, and the stones were installed in about 1827. Sadly, few of Telford's handsome milestones remain.

Of those that still stand, many have lost their cast iron plates, but the distinctive shape of the stones leaves little doubt that they are those designed by Thomas Telford. Two remain in Hertfordshire near St Albans. They have had distances painted on the recessed panel where the metal plate should have been. In Buckinghamshire Telford's stones have been renovated. The plaques seem to have survived World War II, but some were stolen more recently. They were remade using photographs of the originals as a guide. In some places the original red sandstone posts have been replaced by stronger Cornish granite. One can be seen at Fenny Stratford. Another stone which has recently had its metal plate replaced stands on the outskirts of Daventry (Northants), although sadly the other milestones along the A45 between Daventry and its junction with the A5 all have their plates missing. One that hopefully still has the metal plate stands one and a half miles west of Shrewsbury and reads 105 miles to Holyhead and 1 mile 6 furlongs to Salop. Others can be seen near Oswestry. Ten miles east of Bangor on the Welsh section of the road, one of Telford's milestones has become the traditional starting point for a rock climb up Milestone Buttress. The Holyhead road through the Nant Ffrancon Pass was widened in the 1970s and Gwynedd County Council stored the milestone away for safe-keeping while the work was in progress. When the time came to re-erect it, it was found that the metal plate had disappeared. A replica was cast, but a few years later this also vanished. Some of the milestones on the Welsh section of the road do, thankfully, survive intact. The design Telford used for his tollhouses was widely copied, and similar buildings can be found in other areas of the country. The Shelton Tollhouse from the Holyhead road has been re-erected at Blists Hill Museum, Ironbridge (Salop) along with tollgates which were found in Wales, and a milestone which once stood at Knockin Hill west of Shrewsbury **(26)**.

Rebus Posts
A rebus is a pun or picture puzzle originating from the days when most of the population was illiterate. Some of the most

unusual milestones in the country must be the rebus posts of East Sussex. The Bow Bells series, as they are usually called, show the mileage figures to London, a bow and five bells of decreasing size (**27**). These cast iron plates, usually bolted to wooden posts, but sometimes to a wall, can be found mainly along the A22 from Lingfield (Surrey) to Hailsham (Sussex), and the A26 from Uckfield to Lewes (Sussex). The posts were put up, probably in the late eighteenth century, by three turnpike trusts along these roads: London to Wych Cross, Lewes to Wych Cross, and Uckfield to Langney Bridge, northeast of Eastbourne.

27 *Isfield (Sussex)*   **28** *Wych Cross (Sussex)*

Since about 1958 East Sussex County Council has renovated the original posts and has had new ones cast at local foundries to replace those that were missing. Closer inspection will reveal several differences between the posts. Most have a large black boss above the mileage, but some of those between Uckfield and Hailsham show the Pelham buckle, probably as a tribute to the Pelham family where the roads crossed their estates. Several members of the family were also trustees of these turnpikes. There are several variations of the story of how this symbol came to be incorporated into the family's coat of arms, though all begin at the battle of Poitier in 1356. Perhaps the most charming version is that Sir John de Pelham, the youngest of the knights to capture the French king, John, was left out when the spoils of war were distributed. An older knight took pity on him and gave him the king's buckle. On recently recast mileposts the buckle has been replaced by a shield with three vertical lines on it.

At Wych Cross there are two 35-mile posts about half a mile apart. In the late eighteenth century the route of the London to Wych Cross Turnpike was altered to avoid a steep hill at Godstone. This added about half a mile to the route and the turnpike trustees moved their milestones accordingly. The trustees of the Wych Cross to Lewes Turnpike, however, refused to move their posts, which meant that a new post had to be made for the former turnpike. Whether the original mould had been lost, or whether the trustees just decided to use a completely different pattern is unknown, but the extra post has a stylised flower design above and below the mileage **(28)**. Although it looks very attractive, it gives travellers no idea where they are going. An article published in 1961 shows the second 35-mile post to be of the Bow Bells series with a small figure of a man hanging from the lower bell, possibly to denote the site of a gibbet.[14] In the early 1980s the milepost vanished. The article also noted that when the rebus posts were removed in 1940 it took two strong men to carry each one.

Cast Iron
Early in the 1800s cast iron began to appear in more diverse forms in the street and as the century progressed our towns sprouted lamp standards (first for gas and later for electric lights), bollards, drinking fountains, pillar boxes and many other items of street furniture. The first milestones to be made entirely of cast iron probably appeared in the second decade of the nineteenth century. The most popular basic shape was a V-plan post with sloping triangular top and a vertical headplate. It was simple, strong and economical and presented four surfaces for showing information. On many posts the maker's name has also been cast, giving added local interest **(5,29,30,35,62)**,

and some also show a date (**29,62**). Cast iron was very versatile and there are many variations on the V-plan shape. It was easy to make them more decorative, and they can be found with a great variety of lettering styles and with embellishments such as a coat of arms (**36**), pointing hands (**8**), or arrows.

The majority of cast iron mileposts to be found today are of the V-plan shape with a vertical headplate. Some of the oldest can be seen in Suffolk on the A144 south of Bungay. One of the easiest to see is at Bramfield where the post is set in a pavement. The name of the parish and the distance to London is given on the headplate, while the sloping triangular face below it reads 'J. GARRETT/IRON-FOUNDER/ST MARGARET'S/ IPSWICH/1818'. Jacob Garrett was responsible for many other similar mileposts in Suffolk over the next few years (**29**). Posts on the A41 between Tring (Herts.) and Aylesbury (Bucks.) were made by R. J. & J. Barratt in 1826. Several named and dated posts occur in Essex on the road between Colchester and Harwich. The posts must have acted as a good advertisement for their maker, reading 'BENDALL/IRON & BRASS/ FOUNDER/PLOUGH & MACHINE/MAKER/ LAWFORD/ ESSEX/1834'. A well-preserved post in this series can be found in Ardleigh (**62**). At the junction of the Thetford and Bury St Edmunds roads just before they enter Newmarket (Suffolk) stands a milepost cast by Samuel Ridley of 'St Edmund's Bury' and dated 1838. A post with a small elliptical headplate stands north of St Albans (Herts.) on the road to Luton. The headplate carries the name of Brown & Green of Luton, a firm established in 1840.

The variations on these styles are endless. A post at Lower Shuckburgh (Warwicks.) has what might be described as a plunging neckline, the upper face coming down to a long, gradual point and making the milepost look more slender and elegant. It was made by James Tarver of Sheaf Street, Daventry for the Northampton to Warwick Turnpike. Posts with a 'dished' or slightly concave headplate tend to look wider and sturdier, the bulldogs of the genre. Several of this type stand along the A625 from the outskirts of Sheffield to Chapel-en-le-

Frith (Derbys.). A much plainer version can be seen at Sutton Bridge (Lincs.). Barwell & Co. of Northampton made mileposts of this shape for the Wellingborough to Newport Pagnell road. One still stands near Warrington (Bucks.) but the trademark of the firm - an eagle on a shield - is no longer clearly defined. Seymour of Aylesbury made the post at Haddenham (Bucks.), one of a series between Aylesbury and Thame.

29 Gorleston (Norfolk)   *30 Gt Bentley (Essex)*

London has several examples of mileposts with a shorter, more rounded headplate, and one stands just behind the railings outside the Milestone Hotel in Kensington. 'KENSINGTON PARISH' is cast around the top, with 'HOUNSLOW/8^1/2' on the left-hand face and 'LONDON/ 1^1/2' on the right-hand. By the early nineteenth century 170 coaches a day passed along this road on their way to Exeter, Bath, Gloucester and Oxford. Another milepost of this design is on the edge of Ealing Common on the Uxbridge road.

The above examples all have a rounded headplate, but some mileposts have a headplate coming to a point at the top, giving them a more angular appearance. Wootton Bros. Ironworks in Coalville were responsible for many posts of this style in Leicestershire, but as the brothers - William, John and Albert - did not set up their foundry until 1876, these posts are relatively recent. Examples can be found along the A512 from Loughborough towards Burton-upon-Trent, and in Breedon on the Hill. Some of the lettering is arched, some horizontal. All have the parish name on the headplate. The maker's cast mark can be found on an oval plaque on the triangular sloping face. At Morcott (Leics./Rutland) two posts with pointed headplates, but no sign of a maker's name, can be found within a few yards of each other. The post on the A47 belonged to the Leicester-Wansford-Peterborough Turnpike, while that on the A6121 comes from the Stamford-Greetham Turnpike. A series on the Hatfield to St Albans Road (Herts.) was made by Wilder & Sons of Reading for the Hatfield to Reading Turnpike, probably in the 1820s. Stanford & Co. of Colchester made the post on the A133 at Great Bentley (Essex) **(30)**. The lettering on the side faces forms a circle around the figures, and the traveller is left in no doubt as to his whereabouts as Great Bentley is mentioned three times.

Cast iron mileposts of the V-plan shape without a headplate are not quite so common and judging by those which can be dated were mostly made in the latter half of the nineteenth century **(7,8,57)**. Several can be seen in Staffordshire, particularly those associated with the Burton-upon-Trent to Abbots Bromley Turnpike. The parish name is given on the upper face. Another of the same design stands in Alstonefield. On the slip road leading on to the A14 from Godmanchester (Cambs.) the post has a black border and the town names are arched over the mileage. There are several more in the series between Godmanchester and Cambridge, but they are not easily seen. A post with attractive lettering stands at Otterington (Yorks.). Because of the length of the town names they have had to be abbreviated to 'NO'ALLERTON' and 'BORO'BRIDGE'.

Sometimes the lettering looks as though it has been cast on raised panels. Instead of an individual pattern being made for each milepost, one pattern for the basic shape was used and separate small patterns were added to each mould to form the inscription, thus making their manufacture easier and cheaper. A post of this type stands at Nettlebridge (Somerset), the panels having cut-away edges. It gives distances to Cheltenham, Shepton Mallet and Bath and was erected by the Shepton Mallet Turnpike Trust, probably in the late 1830s. The Wells Turnpike Trust used a similar design as demonstrated by the post at Coxley (Somerset). As space was restricted by the raised panels, two of the destinations had to be abbreviated to GLASTON and B/WATER.

The series of mileposts between Sherborne and Shaston (Shaftesbury, Dorset) just have the mileage figures on a raised panel. These posts have a flattened 'spine' on which is cast the parish name. Note the change of spelling of West Stour - Stower in the milepost - nine miles from Sherborne. A very unusual milepost can be seen opposite the church in Earls Colne (Essex). The sans serif lettering is on raised oval rings.

In a series of posts made for the Radstock Turnpike Trust, the upper face comes to a point at the top. These can be seen between Kilmersdon and Norton St Philip (Somerset). A variation on the simple V-plan post has a smaller V-plan stem. Several can be found in the Christchurch (Hants) area, notably along the A338 to Fordingbridge. The maker's name (Joseph J. Armfield of Ringwood) is cast diagonally down the stem. This style can also be seen in Herefordshire along the A40 between Ross-on-Wye and the Welsh border, and at Hardwicke between Hay-on-Wye and Peterchurch. One made for the Poole Turnpike Trust stands at Edmondsham (Dorset).

Although it was the most common style, the V-plan milepost was by no means the only shape made in cast iron. Club-shaped, or 'bobbin-top' posts are mainly restricted to Cheshire, Derbyshire and Staffordshire, and make a pleasant change from the conventional styles. Their main disadvantage was that the amount of space for displaying the town name was limited, making abbreviations necessary. The series of posts along the A537 between Buxton (Derbys.) and Macclesfield (Cheshire) had to have the destination shortened to 'MACCL^D' to fit it in. The long 'stem' did, however, give room for the maker's name - J. Harrison of Derby. The original turnpike road was created in 1759, but because it incorporated many steep gradients on the climb to 1,690 feet at the Cat and Fiddle Inn, a new road was created in 1821 which, although slightly longer, used gentler slopes. The modern main road uses the route of the later turnpike, while the 1759 route can still be followed on minor roads and footpaths. John Harrison of

Bridge Gate, Derby was also responsible for posts on the Duffield to Derby road, that standing outside Two Mile Cottage in Allestree having attractively curly figure twos.

A fine series of fifteen bobbin-top posts still stands along the Ashbourne (Derbys.) to Leek (Staffs.) road. They were made for the turnpike by James Bassett of Ashbourne in 1834 **(31)**. The distance to London is given on the stem. Some of the Derbyshire turnpike trusts used an economy model with only the name 'London' cast around the top. All other towns and mileages had to be painted on, but unfortunately in recent years this practice has not been continued, and most of them are blank and rusty. A post in reasonable condition can be seen beside a bus shelter in Ashford in the Water, and one of the few which has been kept in good repair with destinations painted on stands at the junction of the A619 and B6012 near Baslow. Another variation of this design

31 *Morridge Side (Staffs.)*

88

occurs in Cheshire, with the destinations carried on a rectangular panel cast on to a cylindrical post, looking somewhat like a lectern. These can be seen particularly around Knutsford, and a good series stands along the A537 to Macclesfield. The foundry of Smith Patterson & Co of Blaydon (Northumb.) was responsible for two unusual designs. An example of one of them can be found near Hedgeley. It has a sloping shield on a cylindrical post and the two destinations - Cornhill (on Tweed) and Morpeth - have arrows to point the way. Further down the post is a small rectangular plaque reading 'W/10', standing for Wooler. The second design has an oval top with faceted twin faces on a circular fluted shaft. A series stands between Alnwick and Chatton, with a good specimen to be found at Denwick, one mile from Alnwick (**32**). Another series of this pattern is on the road from Alnwick to North Sunderland.

32 *Denwick (Northumb.)*

Beside the A603 at Barton south of Cambridge stands a small, tombstone-shaped cast iron post with gabled top and hollow back. It only gives the mileage to Cambridge and has the parish name cast near the base. An interesting variation on the V-plan shape occurs in Cumbria. The two side faces are slightly concave and the top is domed. One dated 1825 can be seen at Leagate between Shap and Kendall, and another, dated 1900, near Brigsteer (**33**). The latter may be a replacement for an earlier post. On the main roads leading out of Sherborne (Dorset) large, rectangular mileposts with pedimented tops can be found marking one mile. They are about four feet high and were made for the Sherborne Turnpike Trust. A very similar post can be found one mile from Wells (Somerset) giving distances to Glastonbury and Bridgewater, and there are several in the vicinity of Warminster (Wilts.). The shape may mimic a local style in headstones. The posts in Wiltshire were made by Carson & Miller of Warminster in about 1840 (**34**).

 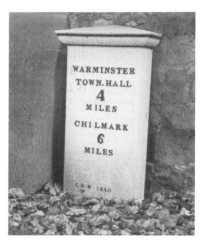

33 Brigsteer (Cumbria)   *34 Tytherington (Wilts.)*

It was relatively easy to add decoration to cast iron mileposts. At Chatteris (Cambs.) a slender V-plan post gives distances to London, Wisbech and St Ives (**35**). It stands on a square plinth which bears the parish name. On the rounded headplate two crossed keys have been cast. The post was made for the Chatteris-Wisbech-Downham Market and the Wisbech-Cross Keys Wash Turnpikes. Another post in this series stands near Outwell (Norfolk) on the road towards Downham Market. The maker's name and address have been cast on the back of the posts - J.N.S. Sturgess & Co. Bowling Ironworks, near Bradford, Yorkshire. It is most unusual to find nineteenth-century cast iron mileposts made by a company so far away; usually local foundries were used.

Coats of arms add an attractive embellishment, and several mileposts in Leicestershire have a lion and unicorn crest (36). Those on the road between Lutterworth and Market Harborough were made by Joseph Illston at Victoria Foundry, Leicester. The post in this series near Walcote is dwarfed by a large, modern signpost. A few also stand beside the Leicester to Welford road. During World War II they were buried in the roadside verges and were later recovered with the aid of a mine detector. Another post with a very elaborate coat of arms stands against the wall of the Royal Geographical Society in Knightsbridge (London). This large milepost is dated 1911 and also has hands pointing the way to Hounslow and Hyde Park Corner. The arms are those of the City of Westminster. The rose of Yorkshire is cast on the headplate of a post on the village green at Anderby Steeple. Bold arrows point the way to Northallerton, Bedale and Hawes.

 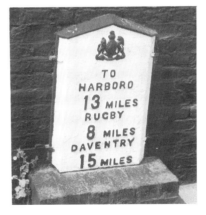

35 Chatteris (Cambs.)   *36 Lutterworth (Leics.)*

A V-plan post with a rather truncated headplate stands a quarter of a mile from the centre of Lutterworth (Leics.) on the Coventry road. All the lettering is cast on raised panels of different shapes, while the maker's name - Cort Paul & Cornick,

91

Leicester - is cast in a circle around a stylised flower. The post in the Museum of Staffordshire Life at Shugborough was originally made for the Newcastle to Uttoxeter road by Thornewill of Burton-on-Trent in 1828. It also shows the distance to London, using very ornate lettering. The Westerham and Edenbridge Turnpike Trust (Kent) erected a series of flat, slender cast iron mileposts, probably in the late eighteenth century. They just show the mileage to London, but the name of the capital snakes from left to right down the post. The turnpike extended to Ashdown Forest (Sussex). A very decorative milepost, stolen in the late 1990s, stood on the Wigan to Preston road in Charnock-Richard (Lancs.). The rectangular metal plate with arched top had the inscription arched to match. Swags of foliage were cast below the lettering and there was further ornamentation on top. The inscription also indicated that it was made at Haigh Foundry in 1837.

Surprisingly few pointing hands are found on cast iron milestones, but can be seen on a series between Malton and York (Yorks.). Triangular plan posts erected by some of the Highway Districts in Yorkshire at the end of the nineteenth century have pointing hands. Posts at Swinithwaite and Sedbusk have already been mentioned in Chapter 2, and there are others of the same design to be found in the county. The flat post at Greinton (Somerset) has very small, rudimentary hands, and was cast by J. Culverwell & Co of Bridgwater.

The small wayside milestones described here represent just a few of the many thousands still to be found beside English roads and serve to illustrate the immense variety of shapes and styles that were used in the eighteenth and nineteenth centuries.

CHAPTER 5

Milestones in England:
Long, Short and Tall

Many milestones are large, spectacular structures, but because the popular image of a milestone is of a small object standing beside the highway, the larger ones are often assumed to be some other kind of memorial and their primary purpose is overlooked. Most of the large milestones were put up privately, and because of this it is often easier to find out their date and history. Many reflect the life or eccentricities of the person responsible for building them and mirror the architectural fashion of the time. Some had a dual purpose, besides showing mileage. Distances on a mounting block are understandable, but why should they be found on a memorial to a battle? Because of their size and historic background, most of these large structures are safe from over-zealous developers and are not in such danger of damage as their smaller wayside cousins.

Mileage markers on walls are not always obvious, especially when the distances are inscribed on a stone at first floor level, ideal for travellers on horseback but hidden from the car-bound. They are most likely to be found in towns, particularly along old coaching routes. Milestones were also tucked out of the way on the parapets of bridges so as not to obstruct the roadway.

New milestones are still being made and it is encouraging to see pedestrians and cyclists once again being catered for by the siting of new stones on long-distance paths.

Obelisks

From the mid-eighteenth to the early nineteenth century the obelisk was very popular in the fashion for neo-classical architecture, and many were erected for different purposes, including milestones. The formal definition of an obelisk is a tapering column, square in section and pyramidal at the top. The design originated in ancient Egypt where they were placed at the entrance to temples of the sun.

37 *Southwark (London)*   **38** *Tixall (Staffs.)*

Obelisk milestones come in many assorted sizes. Some are small and stout, while others taper gracefully to forty or fifty feet (12.2-15.2 m). They can have more than four sides and are occasionally topped with an ornament such as a ball or an urn. One of the finest and oldest obelisk milestones stands in Southwark (London) outside the Imperial War Museum (**37**). One inscription informs us that it was erected in 1771, the eleventh year of the reign of King George III, while another gives the name of the Lord Mayor - The Right Honourable Brass

Crosby Esquire. It gives very precise distances of one mile from Palace Yard Westminster, one mile XXXX feet from London Bridge and one mile CCCC feet from Fleet Street. These distances are no longer accurate, however, because the 40 ft (12.2 m) high obelisk had to be moved from its original site in St George's Circus in 1905 to make way for a clock tower. In earlier times, however, it was an important landmark. Several turnpikes leading into Surrey and Sussex had tollgates at St George's Circus, and these were often referred to as the obelisk tollbars. The column was adorned with lamps to illuminate these busy tollgates at night for the safety of travellers. The obelisk could also serve as a memorial to Alderman Brass Crosby who was imprisoned in 1771 because he freed the printer who had been arrested for printing the debates of the politician John Wilkes. Although an elected MP, Wilkes was barred from taking his seat in Parliament because of his radical views. He had been arrested several times for libel. Crosby was released after six months but died soon afterwards.

On the approach to Richmond Bridge (London) stands a much smaller obelisk about 15 ft (4.5 m) in height and the information inscribed on it would have taken a traveller some time to absorb. It tells us that the first stone of the bridge was laid on 23rd August 1773 and that construction was finished in December 1777. This inscription uses the upright s, and therefore probably predates the much less elaborate lettering on the other two faces. Very exact distances are given to eleven destinations within fifteen miles, for example 'TO LONDON/Bridge/XI Miles/one Quarter' and 'STAINES/IX Miles/and Half' and ends with a statement from the Commissioners that anyone wilfully damaging the obelisk will be prosecuted. A toll was charged to cross the bridge until 1859 and Pastor Moritz, while on his walking holiday in England in 1782, had to pay 1d.

A slender obelisk about 10 ft (3 m) high stands beside a roundabout near St Ives (Cambs.). In 1965 it was found broken and being used as a gatepost and was then repaired and replaced in its original position. Some of the lettering is ornamented with long flourishes, and the faces are adorned with pointing hands carved in relief. It marks one end of the St Ives to Somersham Turnpike which was created in 1765. Another obelisk, dated 1773, stands at the other end of the former turnpike, but this one shows no mileages.

Drivers on the M1 in south Yorkshire who can spare a few seconds to glance eastwards just north of junction 36 will see the top of a dark stone obelisk. It was built in 1775 for one of the Earls of Strafford and it records three miles to their estate at Wentworth Castle. Those who take a detour to Birdwell for a closer look will find probably the tallest milestone in Britain soaring to about 60 ft (18.3 m). Sadly this imposing monument is now squeezed between a row of cottages, an oil tank, and a vehicle repair workshop built on the quarry which produced the stone for the obelisk. The incongruously small mileage plaque was replaced in the 1960s when the old inscription had worn away, and the top of the column was struck by lightning at the end of the nineteenth century and had to be repaired.

A graceful, hexagonal obelisk about 20 ft (6 m) high can be seen at a road junction in the village of Tixall (Staffs.) (**38**). The stone is from the same quarry as that used to build the bridge across the river Severn at Worcester. Dated 1776, it shows $3^{1}/_{2}$ miles to Stafford, 12 to Lichfield and 131 to London. The mileages are at rider's eye level, and above the Stafford distance someone has carved 'H.C. 1886' into the stone. To have reached that height for his carving, H.C. must have been mounted on a horse! The nearby estate was owned by the Clifford family. Perhaps H.C. was one of them. Another hexagonal obelisk stands in Dunchurch (Warwicks.). In 1813 it was placed on the site of the shaft of an old market cross which had been destroyed during the Reformation. It is on the route of the old coaching road to Holyhead and what Pevsner describes as an inscribed waistband gives distances of 79 miles to London and 178 to Holyhead. It was renovated in 1953 to celebrate the coronation, and again in 1977 to mark the Queen's Silver Jubilee.

When it was first erected, the obelisk at Chalfont St Peter (Bucks.) must have been very spectacular. It was originally 60 ft (18.3 m) high but has been reduced to half that height by lightning strikes in 1879 and the early 1960s. It was built in 1785 by Sir H. T. Gott who lived at nearby Newland. The *Handbook for Buckinghamshire* (1903) states that the obelisk was put up to commemorate George III seeing a stag killed on that spot while he was out hunting, but a local story alleges that it was erected as a result of the king becoming lost while riding in the surrounding forest. It would certainly have been visible above the trees when at its full stature. It is built of flint rubble, and a stone slab on one side, at horseback height, tells us it is I Mile III Furlongs to Newland, VII Miles to Chesham, IV to Denham, VI to Uxbridge and XXI to London.

Two much smaller obelisks can be found in Suffolk. At about 10 ft (3 m) in height, that in Nayland has a stone ball on top and shows 55 miles to London and distances to four other towns in Suffolk, including Hadleigh, in a variety of lettering styles. On the opposite side of the road is an old coaching inn whose customers would no doubt have found the milestone useful. In Hadleigh another obelisk gives distances to Suffolk towns in Roman numerals, but the 64 miles to London in Arabic numerals **(39)**. The local rector repaired the milestone in about 1892 and was advised to plug the letters with lead to preserve them. Traces of the lead can still be seen.

The obelisk dated 1808 at Bredon (Her. & Worcs.) has the towns arranged down the column with the shortest name (Upton) occupying the narrowest part at the top and the longest name (Cheltenham) at the base. The six towns listed in attractive lettering are on cast iron plates fixed to the column. In the Market Place, Marlow (Bucks.) is an obelisk erected by the Trustees of the Reading and Hatfield Road in September 1822. The turnpike was said to have been created to shorten the journcy of members of the Cecil family from Hatfield to join the London to Bath turnpike at Reading. They are reputed to have travelled to Bath frequently to take the waters, and the road was thus popularly known as the 'Gout Track'. Among the dozen destinations listed on three of the sides is 80 miles to Bath. Towns as far afield as Edinburgh (295 miles), Plymouth (205 miles), and Portsmouth (163 miles) are shown on the obelisk at Craven Arms (Salop), proving that this was an important road junction. Local places also feature among the thirty-six destinations listed. The town takes its name from the coaching inn opposite the milestone.

39 *Hadleigh (Suffolk)*   **40** *Esher (Surrey)*

The 7 ft (2.1 m) high obelisk in Snaresbrook (London) stands where the road from Whitechapel forks to Epping and to Ongar. Known locally as The Highstone, the square stone base on which it stands is thought by some to be Roman. The obelisk was moved to its present site in the 1960s during road alterations. The inscription has become very eroded and the rear face is indecipherable, but earlier descriptions record it as giving distances to Whitechapel, The Standard in Cornhill and Hyde Park Corner. The Eagle at Snaresbrook was a busy coaching inn on the routes to East Anglia.

Monuments

Apart from obelisks, other large milestones, that is those over about 5 ft (1.5 m) in height, come in a great variety of shapes and sizes and it is difficult to say what influenced their design. They were usually erected by a local landowner or benefactor, probably more with an eye to self-publicity than to sympathy for the common traveller. Some of these monuments have acquired picturesque names.

Most descriptions of the 'White Lady' put it outside the Orleans Arms in Esher (Surrey) **(40)**. By the mid-1990s the inn had become the Café Rouge and the 10 ft (3 m) high cylindrical column topped with a ball was a dirty brown. It was erected beside the Portsmouth road in 1767 by the Duke of Newcastle to guide visitors, and particularly messengers from George III when the Duke was Prime Minister, to his country house at Claremont. It gives distances to seventeen places including Portsmouth and Haslemere, Hampton Court, Westminster Bridge and Hyde Park Corner.

'Holt Obelisk' is a misnomer, because the square-sectioned stone pillar topped by a foliated ball is certainly not the correct shape. However, it always seems to have been known by this name, and is thus marked on Faden's map of Norfolk published in 1797. It is reputed to have been a gatepost from nearby Melton Constable Hall and was given to the market town of Holt in the mid-eighteenth century by Sir Edward Astley who was MP for the area. Mileages to other Norfolk towns are shown on three sides, but the fourth gives distances to nearby country estates such as Blickling, Holkham, Houghton and Felbrigg Halls. Its twin gatepost was donated to the town of East Dereham eighteen miles away, but sadly 'Dereham Obelisk' was destroyed in 1946 when the road layout was altered and a war memorial placed on the spot.

Adjacent to the eastern carriageway of the A1M at Alconbury Hill (Cambs.) is a square pillar topped by a spire and ball and protected by iron railings. It marked the intersection of the Great North Road and the Old North Road and alternative routes and mileages to London - via Huntingdon, Cambridge and Biggleswade - are indicated on it by pointing hands. Until the late 1990s when this part of the A1 became a motorway, the milepost stood in the central reservation of the dual carriageway. Modern traffic makes it too dangerous to take a close look, and a letter in *Country Life* in 1952 records that this eighteenth-century milestone has been hit by vehicles at least once. An elaborate, square, Victorian pillar stands by the A3400 just north of Newbold on Stour (Warwicks.). Put up in 1871, it gives the mileage in verse:

6 Miles
To Shakespeare's Town whose Name
Is known throughout the Earth
To Shipston 4 whose Lesser Fame
Boasts no such Poet's Birth.

A slender sandstone shaft, tapering downwards, can be found outside the main entrance to Sheffield Park (Sussex). It is just over 9 ft (2.7 m) high and mileages are inscribed at the top on three sides. It shows distances to East Grinstead and Lewes in Roman numerals, and to Westminster Bridge, East Grinstead, Lewes and Brighthelmstone (Brighton) in Arabic numerals. Sheffield Park House was completed for the 1st Earl of Sheffield in 1779, and it is probable that this milestone was put up at his instruction the following year.

A milestone that does reflect something of its architect's character stands near West Wycombe (Bucks.) **(41)**. Sir Francis Dashwood, founder of the Hellfire Club, was a man of many talents and interests who went out of his way to be different from his contemporaries. After a succession of poor harvests he tried to alleviate the hardship caused to families in the area by employing them to build a new road from West Wycombe to High Wycombe. When the road was completed in 1752 'The Pedestal' was erected at the junction with the Aylesbury road. The cylindrical, slightly tapering column is mounted on a square plinth and is topped by a square slab and a stone ball. The distances are carved on the sides of the square slab, and a traveller would have needed to be mounted on quite a large horse to get close enough to read them. Even then he might not have known that 'The City' meant London, 'The County Town' was Aylesbury, and 'The University' was Oxford. This has also been called a shy milestone because of the cryptic destinations.

41 *West Wycombe (Bucks.)*   **42** *Markham Moor (Notts.)*

Just off the A6 at Desborough (Northants), in front of a modern parade of shops, stands a slender stone pillar about 15 ft (4.5 m) high topped by a ball. The inscriptions, at rider's-eye level, are not easily read today, but the distance of 81 miles from London is fairly clear. Very few travellers nowadays must pass the strange fluted, cast iron column beside a country lane near Raveningham Hall (Norfolk), home of the Bacon family. It stands about 10 ft (3 m) high with castellated top and near the base bronze plaques give the distance to London of 111 miles. On either side is the coat of arms of the Bacon family - a boar with fleur-de-lis. Against the brick plinth a slate tablet states that the monument was erected by Sir Edmund Bacon in 1831 and

101

restored in 1986 to commemorate the birth of Edmund Anthony Bacon.

Only a few letters can now be made out on the oval-plan stone column at Markham Moor (Notts.) (**42**). The Great North Road once passed this 7 ft 6 in (2.3 m) milestone, but the A1 has now been diverted. A few miles further north the Great North Road took various routes at different periods of its history.[1] Mail-coach services, which started in about 1785, used the road through Retford but, before this, the route passed to the west of the town and it can still be traced today along lanes and bridleways. Between Gamston and the present A1 is a rectangular stone about 5 ft (1.5 m) high with pedimented top. Inscriptions on three sides read: 'From/London 142/Miles/and half; Coach Road to/Work*f*op Mannor/Hou*f*e/7 Miles 3 chs/176-; The Keys/at the Jockey/Hou*f*e'. Worksop Manor was burnt down in 1761 and rebuilt four years later. Perhaps this milestone was to guide travellers on the Great North Road to the new House. A turnpike gate once stood here, and presumably the keys to it could be obtained at the inn. *White's Directory* for Nottinghamshire states that the Jockey House was once a noted inn but by 1885 had become a farmhouse. The house, much altered, still stands opposite the stone.

Two milestones about 12 ft (3.6 m) high stand half a mile apart in Ackworth (Yorks.). The stone columns each have a triangular stone slab at the top with distances along the three edges and hands carved to point the way. The column opposite the Quaker School is dated 1805 and has three wrought iron lamps on top, while the milestone closer to Pontefract has the date 1827 and is ornamented by a stone ball (**43**). The milestone standing on a small green at a road junction in Beckford (Her. & Worcs.) was built to commemorate Queen Victoria's golden jubilee in 1887 (**44**). Although renovated in 1953, the inscriptions round the square base are now badly worn and difficult to read. The slender cylindrical column surmounted by an urn makes the whole structure about ten feet high.

43 *Ackworth (Yorks.)*   **44** *Beckford (Her. & Worcs.)*

Smaller than these, but still larger than most wayside milestones, is the stone standing outside Milestone House in Broadway (Her. & Worcs.). The towns listed are carved in a variety of lettering styles, but a small metal plaque at the base informs us that the stone was defaced in 1939 and restored in 1953.

Multi-purpose Milestones

A block of dressed stone was a valuable commodity and could be put to many uses. If it had a blank surface or two and stood beside a main road, even if its principal function was for something totally different, why not adorn it with the distances to nearby towns?

Many of these multi-purpose milestones did have connections with roads and travellers, and mounting or upping blocks are an obvious example. Edmund Boulter, a corpulent gentleman who lived near Wakefield and who regularly travelled to London on the Great North Road, had considered erecting milestones along his route for the benefit of all travellers.

103

Instead he provided a series of mounting blocks between Stilton and Grantham to ease his overweight body on and off his horse. Only one of the stones survives, near Water Newton (Cambs.), inscribed EB 1704.[1] A milestone at Poringland (Norfolk), whose mileage is no longer legible but was, according to old maps, Norwich 4 Bungay 10, has a stirrup-shaped step cut in the back to aid the rider to climb to the top. Another mounting block-cum-milestone which has lost its inscription stands just outside Dunchurch (Warwicks.). This is in the form of three steps. At Bulls Cross (Glos.) a mounting block supports a metal plate which has probably lost its original stone support. It stands three miles from Stroud on the Cheltenham road. The hamlet of Stone Chair north of Brighouse (Yorks.) takes its name from the seat reputedly provided by William Clayton to encourage stage-coaches to stop at the Duke of York Inn across the road. The present chair consists of two vertical slabs of stone set at right angles with a block of stone in the angle to form the seat. The inscription on the back has hands pointing in the directions of Halifax, Bradford, Denholme Gate and Brighouse and also tells us that the chair was first erected in 1737 and re-erected in 1891. It has no mileages, however. Against the wall of a nearby cottage is a stone from the original chair. The only lettering visible now is 'H...d/17..' but an article by J. J. Brigg in the *Yorkshire Archaeological Journal* in 1930 (see Bibliography) records the inscription as 'Huddersfield Road 6m; Bradford 4m; Keighley 8m; Halifax 2m; William Clayton 1737'. These distances were in customary miles which were longer than the statute mile (see Chapter 3).

The Earl of Upper Ossory had a new water pump erected in the Market Place at Ampthill (Beds.) in 1785 **(45)**. It was encased in a stone obelisk topped by a lantern and was designed by Sir William Chambers, who was Court Architect to George III and who also designed Somerset House in London and the Pagoda in Kew Gardens. The Earl contributed £20 towards sinking a new well to supply the town pump, but the inhabitants had to find the rest of the cost. On the sides of the obelisk are inscribed the distances to the towns reached by the four main roads radiating from the Market Place - London, Dunstable, Woburn and Bedford. The Hon. John Byng mentioned seeing the 'grand pump' when he stayed at the White Hart at Ampthill in 1794 (see Bibliography: *The Torrington Diaries*). Another pump stands at Normanton (Lincs.). This again is a stone obelisk with an iron pull handle at the back and a spout at the front over a stone trough. Distances are given to Lincoln, Grantham and London. The obelisk in the High Street in Cranleigh (Surrey) once served as a drinking fountain. It is dated 1794 and was made by J. Champion. Mileages are given on cast iron plates.

45 *Ampthill (Beds.)*   **46** *Attleborough (Norfolk)*

War memorials have also found use as milestones. A fine obelisk which is known as Hadley Highstone or Barnet Pillar stands just north of Barnet (London). It was erected in 1740 by Jeremy Sambroke who lived at Gobions near North Mimms, but it commemorates the Battle of Barnet during the Wars of the Roses when the Lancastrians were defeated in the early morning mist of an Easter Sunday. An inscription reads

105

'HERE was fought the Famous Battle Between EDWARD the 4th and the Earl of Warwick April the 14th ANNO 1471 in which the Earl was defeated and slain.' The obelisk stands where the old Holyhead road forks left from the Great North Road and the distances, at rider's-eye level, are given to St Albans and Hatfield. Hadley Highstone was a landmark used to time mail-coaches setting off on the two longest main routes in the country. Mail-coach guards were issued with an official timepiece by the Post Office and they were expected to keep a log of their journey. If the coach was delayed by bad weather, the guard could take one of the horses and ride on with the mail. The coaches usually kept to their schedules very well.

What might better be described as a peace memorial stands at a cross-roads in Attleborough (Norfolk) **(46)**. It commemorates the end of the Crimean War and has the names of battles - Inkerman, Alma, Sebastopol and Balaklava - and the date 1856 at the top of the column which is ornamented by a star. Metal brackets once supported lamps, and around the deep plinth at the base are listed distances to twenty-four towns. A small square stone pillar bearing a metal plate reading '130 MILES TO YPRES' stands at Shooter's Hill (London). Below this inscription it informs us that the casualties in defending the Salient were 90,000 killed, 70,500 missing and 410,000 wounded. This milestone was once on the opposite side of the road and bore metal plates indicating 7 miles to Dartford and 8 miles to London Bridge. A writer to *The Gentleman's Magazine* in 1807 commented that 'On the declivity of Shooter's Hill is a milestone, from which the next milestone (on the London road) may be seen. I do not remember whether, but I have met with the same circumstances in another part of the country.' In 1903 the stone was badly damaged by a steamroller but was rescued by the vicar and later repaired and given its present dual purpose and position in front of Christ Church. A concrete milestone was placed on the original site near the Red Lion public house, but its metal plates were probably removed during World War II. With the help of the former Greater London Council, new plates were fitted in 1977.[2]

Other memorials have also doubled as milestones. On the green at Acle (Norfolk) stands a stone commemorating Queen Victoria's Golden Jubilee in 1887. Distances are given to Great Yarmouth by the old, winding turnpike created in 1768, and by the new road known as the Acle Straight which was opened in 1831 and which shortened the distance by three miles. An elegant lamp adorns the top of the stone. The monument was restored in 1980 to commemorate Queen Elizabeth's Silver Jubilee. There must have been a sense of celebration in Haddiscoe (Norfolk) when the Blythburgh to Great Yarmouth road was disturnpiked in 1869 after seventy-four years as a toll road. Ironically, the stone put up to commemorate the event gives the distance, among others, to Haddiscoe Station. It was, after all, the railways that caused the demise of the turnpikes. A much more recent memorial was erected in October 1937 to commemorate the opening of a new road at Urmston (Gt Manchester) by the Vice Chairman of Lancashire County Council. The triangular plan stone stands on a stepped plinth.

It is difficult to know whether the sundial-cum-milestone at Cainscross (Glos.) is entirely original, or whether the sundial was a later addition. The turnpike was created in the mid-eighteenth century and the sundial seems to be dated 1754. A metal plate fixed to the cylindrical base reads 'TO/ STROUD/1/MILE', while inscriptions on the sundial read 'Behold/now/is the/Accepted/TIME' and 'Seek ye/The LORD/ while/he may be/found'.

The boundary stone on the summit of the Trough of Bowland no longer marks the administrative border between Yorkshire and Lancashire. The boundary was moved in 1974 so that the stone is now well inside Lancashire. The destinations on the imposing triangular-plan stone are unusual in that they face the direction from which the traveller has just come and do not indicate the towns that lie ahead.

Walls and Bridges

In towns, where space on the ground in narrow streets was limited, and where a free-standing stone beside the road would have been a danger to horses, carriages and pedestrians, walls provided the ideal site for mileage markers. The most promising places to look for these markers are in old coaching towns where travellers would have commenced their journey along a turnpike, changed coaches, or rested while the team of horses was being changed. It is probable that many inns once had wooden boards outside with mileages painted on them for the benefit of their customers. They would have been cheap to produce, and although not as durable as stone or cast iron, they were easily renewable. Sadly, few survive today, but examples can be found. The sixteenth-century inn at Bradford Abbas (Dorset) may originally have been a rest house for the monks of Sherborne Abbey. The mileage board would seem to cater for walkers as none of the six destinations is more than four miles distant. The board on the wall of the Pied Bull in Northgate Street, Chester, on the other hand, caters for long-distance travellers, listing London (198 miles), Bath (185 miles), as well as Worcester, Ludlow and Bristol. A sign below the board dates it at 1763, although it is surely not the original. The writer George Borrow set off on his journey into 'wild Wales' from here in 1854.

More affluent innkeepers may have provided stone tablets. The mile-long main street of Henley-in-Arden (Warwicks.) still contains several former coaching inns, reflecting the days when the town was an important stopping place on the route from London to Birmingham and Shrewsbury. A black-painted stone is set into the white wall of Milestone Cottage, and reads 'From London/CII Miles/from Stratford/ VIII/To Birmingham/XIV 1748', which seems to assume that travellers are all heading north. Another stone tablet set in the wall of an inn can be seen at the Saracen's Head Hotel in Southwell (Notts.). It gives distances to London, Mansfield and Newark.

A stone tablet was sometimes let into a wall at first floor level. Today's travellers may have difficulty finding it, but the inscription would have been at eye level for anyone on horseback or on top of a stage-coach. A good example can be found in Lewes (Sussex) over the door of a fifteenth-century building now used as a bookshop. The inscription reads: '50 MILES/FROM THE STANDARD/IN CORNHILL/49 TO WESTMINSTER BRIDGE/8 MILES TO BRIGHTHELMSTONE' the latter being the old name for Brighton. It was probably put up in the late eighteenth century.

47 *Oundle (Northants)*

A stone tablet in Castle Street, Cambridge tells us that 'Godmanchester Turnpike Road Ends Here'. A hand pointing to a vertical arrow shows the exact spot. Below is another stone indicating that it is 14 miles 4 furlongs to Horse-ʃhoe Corner, Godmanchester. The road was turnpiked in 1745 and the use of the upright s suggests a mid-eighteenth century date for this stone. The building in whose wall it is placed is now an art gallery, but an inn previously occupied the site. With careful searching a rectangular stone can be seen at first floor level in the wall of a cottage in Thame (Oxon) where the road bends after passing the cattle market. It shows $9^1/2$ miles to Aylesbury with a hand carved in relief pointing the way. Another rectangular stone about seven feet from the ground is set into a wall in Oundle (Northants) beside the narrow, winding main street near the church. The attractive lettering gives 13 miles to 'Peterboro' and $7^3/4$ to Thrapston-Cross. Pointing hands, complete with fingernails, indicate the direction to each town (**47**). The wall of the old court house in High West Street, Dorchester (Dorset) where the Tolpuddle Martyrs were tried in 1834, provides support for a stone showing 120 miles to Hyde Park Corner, along with mileages to Blandford and Bridport.

Not all milestones set into walls are given this lofty position. In the churchyard wall in Holbeach (Lincs.), a stone shows mileages to fourteen towns on its front face, including Great Yarmouth, Birmingham, London and Newark (**48**). On the sides that rise above the brick wall a further four local destinations are given, the wording attractively curved to fit the names into the narrower space. In Dartford Road, Bexley (Kent) a stone set into the base of a wall gives the distance to London Bridge, the traditional starting point for roads into the county. The stone tablet in a brick frame in Wych Cross (Sussex) was originally in the wall of a tollhouse which was demolished in 1965 and may date from the start of the Malling Street to Wych Cross Turnpike in 1752. The inscription reads 'To Maresfield 6 Miles/from Maresfield to Uckfield 1 Mile half/from Uckfield to Lewes 7 Miles half/ And this is the Toll Road to Lewes'.

48 *Holbeach (Lincs.)*

From medieval times, travellers had shortened their journeys between Lancaster and Ulverston by nearly twenty miles by crossing the sands of Morecambe Bay. Because of the dangers involved, guides led travellers over at low tide. Until the opening of local railway lines a daily stage-coach made the journey across the sands, and a relic of this era is the large stone set in a wall in Cartmel (Cumbria) which reads 'LANCASTER/OVER-SANDS 15 MILES/ULVERSTON/ OVER-SANDS 7 MILES' (**49**). In 1811 the *Cumberland Pacquet* reported an accident to the Over Sands coach when the horses became restive, the current washed the sand from under the wheels on one side, and the coach overturned. The fifteen passengers managed to escape but two dogs in the boot could not be rescued before the coach was engulfed by the rising tide. Other travellers were not so lucky and many lost their lives crossing the sands. The narrow road along the eastern side of Lake Windermere (Cumbria) still has a few of its milestones surviving. The stone at Rydal is set into a stone wall while that south of Ambleside is against the wall of a building. William Wordsworth and his son were involved in an accident on this road in 1840 while driving home to Rydal Mount in their gig. They met a mail-coach on the narrow road and their horse took fright and caused the gig to run against the coach, tipping the Wordsworths into a field. Their horse ran away but was eventually stopped at Grassmere turnpike gate.

49 *Cartmel (Cumbria)*   **50** *North Elmham (Norfolk)*

Metal mileage plates were durable and could be attached more easily to walls or to other convenient supports with limited surface area. Many of these markers were probably removed during World War II, but a careful search can reveal a good number still remaining. Some of the plates now fixed to walls may have been attached originally to free-standing stones which have since been lost. Twin metal plates were made in 1838 by E. Cockey of Frome and fixed to a pillar of the Market Cross in Shepton Mallet (Somerset). A flint and brick wall in North Elmham (Norfolk) supports a small rectangular metal plate giving distances of 111 miles to London, 5 to Dereham and 13 to Holt (**50**). The lettering is incised indicating a probable late eighteenth-century date. A simple rectangular plate can be seen on a wall in Swadlincote (Derbys.), and a square plate is situated '01 furlongs' from Ironbridge (Salop). Although the latter looks as though it is attached to a wall, it is in fact on a gable-topped stone post which is now flush with the surrounding brickwork. The metal mileage plate on the outskirts of Torquay (Devon) has been painted with blue lettering and border to match the wall to which it is attached.

In Lutterworth (Leics.) a handsome cast iron plate is fixed to the wall of a former chapel. It shows distances to 'Harboro', Rugby and Daventry and has a lion and unicorn coat of arms cast at the top (**36**). It was almost certainly made by Joseph Illston of Leicester who produced other milestones in the area with a similar decoration (see Chapter 4: Cast Iron). Another plate at ground level stands against a wall beside a busy junction on the A6 in Darley Dale (Derbys.). It shows 146 miles to London, 6 to Bakewell and 4 to Matlock.

The milestone in The Thoroughfare, Woodbridge (Suffolk) is made of cement inside an iron frame and is a twentieth-century replacement for an earlier one. It seems that any wall was convenient for supporting a milestone. A sandstone slab one mile from the centre of Bacup (Lancs.), and showing distances to Burnley and Rochdale, is set into the wall of a urinal.

The parapets of bridges also provided a convenient, out-of-the-way place for mileage markers. Distances to London (100 miles), Stratford-on-Avon, Henley-in-Arden and Birmingham have been carved into the central pillar of the bridge over the river Alne at Wootton Wawen (Warwicks.). The stone is dated 1808, presumably the date the bridge was built. Another milestone over water is built into the parapet of Green Bridge, Richmond (Yorks.). The bridge across the river Swale was built in 1788-89 and the stone shows distances to Askrigg and Lancaster in elegant lettering. Although not set into the stonework of the bridge, the arch-topped, sandstone milestone at Rainhill (Merseyside) is pressed against the brick parapet. The mileages to Warrington, Prescott and Liverpool are given in Roman numerals. The bridge was built in 1829.

Footpaths

Although road vehicles are now progressing too fast for their occupants to notice milestones, there is a new breed of predominantly off-road traveller who is better able to appreciate them - the walker, cyclist and horse-rider. The increasing popularity of these outdoor leisure activities and the proliferation of long-distance footpaths and bridleways has in many places re-opened the old, historic routes across England. The idea of mileage markers beside footpaths is not new. In the early years of the twentieth century the Peak District and Northern Counties Footpaths Preservation Society was erecting cast iron signs on wooden posts in parts of the Pennines. Not all these signs give mileages, but one that does can be found near the bridge at Grindleford (Derbys.). It is painted white on green, and besides giving distances to Bakewell ($6^1/2$ miles) and Sheffield ($9^1/2$ miles), denoting the footpath to Froggatt, Curbar, Calver, Baslow and Chatsworth, it gives the altitude as 427 feet and is dated 1908.

Some of the more recently created long-distance paths have milestones of a more conventional shape. They are not set at every mile, but may occur at a junction of tracks, or have been made to commemorate the opening of the path or its anniversary. Milestones on the Dorset Coast Path are mainly to be found at track junctions. All bear an acorn waymark, and several can be found in the vicinity of Lulworth Cove. A stone on the village green in Balsham (Cambs.) was unveiled in September 1992 to mark the opening of part of the Icknield Way as a long-distance footpath. Mileages are given to its junction with two other ancient tracks - Peddars Way and the Ridgeway - and the stone is decorated with a Stone Age axe, the waymark of the Icknield Way. Also in eastern England a stone standing outside Coggeshall Abbey and marking the half-way point along the Essex Way was unaugurated in 1993 to mark the twenty-first anniversary of the creation of the path (**51**). The emblem of the Council for the Protection of Rural England is carved at the top, and below are distances of 41 miles to Epping and 40 to Harwich. At the eastern end of the path a plaque on the High Lighthouse in Harwich indicates 81 miles to Epping. The beginning (or end) of the Cotswold Way in Chipping Camden (Glos.) is marked by a metal plaque on a stone inscribed 'BATH/100 M' which stands next to the town hall (**52**).

51 Coggeshall (Essex)   *52 Chipping Camden (Glos.)*

It seems surprising that no milestones have been made for the first long-distance path created in Britain - the Pennine Way. Some sort of stone markers, perhaps similar to the old guide stones, would be invaluable in the remoter moorland areas, and would be more durable than wooden signposts.

The charity Sustrans - standing for sustainable transport - was set up in the early 1980s to design and build traffic-free routes for cyclists, walkers and those in wheelchairs. They also had the commendable idea of comissioning mileposts or sculptures to place along the trails. Some of the trails on which these milepost sculptures can be seen are between Consett and Sunderland (Durham), Bristol and Bath, and The Cuckoo Trail between Polegate and Heathfield (Sussex).

The era of the milestone, therefore, is by no means past and there is still scope for erecting practical, informative, or even entertaining markers to measure the way.

CHAPTER 6

Milestone Miscellany

This chapter deals with the oddities to be found by the milestone hunter. Mistakes have crept into the making of milestones, adding a down-to-earth and amusing touch. In some cases abbreviations have been used which would have been very puzzling to travellers unfamiliar with the area, and old names and spellings are a reminder of historical change. Milestones have also been discovered in unlikely locations and it has not always been possible to find out how they came to be in their present resting places.

Redundant milestones have found many varied and imaginative uses. Recycling was widely practised in the past. When the lettering became worn they were often just turned round and the inscription re-cut, and it has already been noted how the Romans changed the inscriptions when a new Emperor came to power (Chapter 4). When no longer needed for their original purpose, these valuable pieces of stone could be put to many other uses.

A final section on theft and vandalism shows that these are by no means modern phenomena, and milestones were among the structures that suffered.

Mistakes and Mysteries

Many workmen in the eighteenth and early nineteenth centuries must have been poorly educated and it is therefore surprising that more mistakes were not made in the lettering of milestones. However, errors can be found and they add humour to the subject. One of the most obvious lapses is the letter S written backwards. This can be seen on a small square pillar near

Zennor (Cornwall) with very crudely carved lettering and a roughly-drawn hand indicating six miles to St Ives. Just north of Cartmel (Cumbria) stands a milestone announcing the distance to Hawkshead, the central S of which has been reversed. A capital N could also cause problems as illustrated by a milestone near Little Swinburn (Northumb.) which has the N of ALNWICK inscribed backwards (**53**). The carver of a stone at Norbury (Salop) forgot about the S altogether to give us 'SHREWBURY/16'.

53 *Little Swinburn*   **54** *Towcester (Northants)*
(Northumb.)

Eight posts remain of a series of cast iron mileposts made for the Norwich to Fakenham Turnpike in Norfolk, probably soon after its inauguration in 1823. The distance to Norwich is given on the vertical headplate, and the parish name is cast on one of the side faces. However, the ironfounder has repeated the Norwich mileage under the parish name on each post so that the milepost at Sparham, for example, indicates that

117

there ought still to be twelve miles to go to that village. Modern sign-painters have left this figure white to avoid confusion.

Other anomalies could be ascribed to a lack of planning on the part of the maker in setting out the inscription and not allowing enough space for all the letters. A stone with cast iron plate at Ranby (Notts.) has had the lettering squeezed to 'RETFOR^D' and 'WORKS^P'. The metal plate at Ironbridge (Salop) has the towns truncated to 'SHREWSB^Y' and 'IRONBR^E'.

Some places were not content with putting just their name on a milestone standing within their boundaries, but wanted to ensure that travellers knew they had arrived by adding '0 Miles' as well. A zero milestone can be seen on the A413 at Winslow (Bucks.) standing against one end of the railway bridge parapet. It also gives distances to London, Banbury, Aylesbury and Buckingham. A stone with cast iron plate in the centre of Mattishall (Norfolk) - one of a series made in 1868 for the Norwich, Swaffham and Mattishall Turnpike - also leaves one in little doubt of one's whereabouts. A V-plan cast iron post giving a zero mileage stands in Fordingbridge (Hants); it was made by Joseph J. Armfield of Ringwood. Another stands against the wall of the George Hotel in the centre of Alfreton (Derbys.). At Pateley Bridge (Yorks.) a long, black finger points down the road despite the zero on the milepost. A cast iron plate on the wall of a house on Watling Street shows travellers that they have indeed reached Towcester (Northants) **(54)**.

Some of the old names and spellings for towns have already been mentioned, and milestones can give a good lesson in the history and evolution of these names. Some names were so different that they are hardly recognisable from their present-day equivalent. The name Brighton only came into common use in the early nineteenth century, the fishing village having previously been called Brighthelmstone. The old name can be found on milestones in Lewes and Sheffield Park (Sussex). Sarum is fairly familiar as the old name for Salisbury, but Barum is probably not readily identifiable with Barnstaple. Both names were from common medieval Latin abbreviations. Milestones on the A377 between Exeter and Barnstaple (Devon) show the destination as Barum on one face of the triangular-plan stones and Exon on the other, the latter name being derived from the Anglo-Saxon Exanceaster (**55**). Thomas Hardy made use of many of these names in his Wessex novels; he called Exeter 'Exonbury'. The name Lanson on a milestone at Little Comfort (Cornwall) may reflect the local pronunciation of Launceston. The town's name is said to be derived from the old Cornish word *lan* meaning a church (**6**). Shaston is an old contraction of the name Shaftesbury, another name used by Thomas Hardy. The Romano-British name Venta became the Old English Wintanceaster. Hardy called Winchester 'Wintoncester', and the name Winton is still found on milestones in Hampshire (**21**).

55 *Copplestone (Devon)*   **56** *Torquay (Devon)*

Travellers in the west country can amuse themselves by counting the variations on the name Gloucester: Glou^r (near Nympsfield), Glocе*f*ter (Painswick), Glos'ter (Cam), GLOS$\underline{R}$ (Nailsworth). At the other side of England a more phonetically accurate 'Wisbeach' has been cast on a milepost at Welney (Norfolk), and many other minor changes of spelling can be found.

Towns with long names must have caused problems for the stonemasons and pattern makers. Some of the old names such as Winton (Winchester) and Soton or Southton (Southampton) probably continued in use on milestones long after they had ceased to be used in common speech just because they could be fitted more easily into the space available (**21**). Other towns, however, were shortened in other ways. Devon has some particularly difficult names to deal with. On a stone two furlongs south of Moretonhampstead, this town is reduced to Moreton, Newton is minus the Abbot and Bovey is without Tracey (**11**). Okehampton is contracted to 'Oke' on some of the stones between that town and Tavistock along the A386, and Plymouth becomes 'Plym^{o}' on a stone near Lipton Hill. A milestone near Worksop (Notts.) on the A60 gives distances to WOR, LON and DON (i.e. Worksop, London and Doncaster). A little more imagination has been used on the cast iron plates bolted to wooden posts on the A35 between Lyndhurst and Christchurch (Hants). BOURNE for Bournemouth is easily guessed, but X^{T}CHURCH for Christchurch is somewhat more cryptic. A very erudite stonemason in Devon has used the Greek letter theta to abbreviate Teignmouth to TEIGNM$^{\theta}$. The stone stands seven miles away in Torquay (**56**).

In some parts of England just the initial letter of the town was used. These posts tend to occur in areas furthest from London and the home counties where travellers were more likely to be local people who would be able to guess what the letter stood for. Cornwall has many good examples. Callington was located at a major cross-roads. On stones to the south-east along the A388 the S stands for Saltash, while on the A390 to the east T means Tavistock and to the west L means Liskeard. In Hampshire a series of milestones on the A337 between Lymington and Christchurch show L for Lymington. While the reason for the Cornish abbreviations might be the difficulty of carving on hard granite, this could not have been the case at the other end of the country where sandstone was used. Small milestones with angled faces and rounded backs mark the A6079 between Rothbury and Hexham (Northumb.). The destinations are inscribed as R.B and H (17). In the same county are cast iron posts also giving just initial letters of the towns. Posts between Morpeth and Alnwick (M and A) are now mostly to be found along the old A1 and not on the modern road. Another series gives distances to A and B (Alnwick and Belford) (57). All these posts are difficult to locate, but perhaps the easiest to see is 'A/1;B/13' which stands against a wall on the Alnwick side of the old A1 roundabout. Similar abbreviations can be found on mileposts in Co. Durham. Near Easington is one recording 'S^D 9; S^M 14' (Sunderland and Seaham).

57 *Denwick (Northumb.)*   **58** *Ingoldisthorpe (Norfolk)*

One of a series of semi-cylindrical stones can be found just west of Dent (Cumbria) on the road leading to Sedbergh along Dentdale. It states, very curtly, 'S/5'. Similarly shaped stones are also positioned along the road between Sedbergh and Askrigg. Some of the inscriptions are now worn away, but a readable example stands east of Sedbusk (Yorks.) inscribed 'A/3; S/17'. In places along this road a cast iron milepost was put opposite the old stone by the local highway district, probably at the end of the nineteenth century. The two generations of milestone can best be seen at Sedbusk close to Mile House Farm, although the inscription on the old stone has now gone.

Occasionally just a mileage is given on the stone with no indication at all as to the destination. On the road between Lancaster and Clitheroe through the Trough of Bowland (Lancs.) the milestones give the distance to Lancaster. At Ingoldisthorpe (Norfolk) the bold metal figure ten on a stone post refers to King's Lynn (**58**).

While collecting material for this book puzzles have cropped up which it has not been possible to solve. Hopefully someone living closer to the milestone concerned with more opportunity to delve into historical records may, in the future, be able to come up with the answers. There is, for instance, a milestone at Lexden (Essex) which was unearthed in 1990 during reconstruction work to the exterior of a church.[1] On one side of the stone the distances of 'Whitham/12' and 'Colcefter/2' are recorded, with the figure 49 at the top, presumably meaning to London. Today's mileage to London is about 52 miles, measured to the datum point in Trafalgar Square, but in the past roads to eastern England were usually measured from Whitechapel. The other mileages are correct. The style of the lettering strongly suggests an eighteenth-century milestone, and in 1726 several earlier turnpike roads were amalgamated to form one from Whitechapel to Harwich via Shenfield. On the reverse of the milestone is another inscription in more modern lettering reading '30.M/FROM/ LONDON/1 FROM/CHELM/-FORD'. If it had stood south of Chelmsford, these distances would be correct. This seems to suggest, therefore, that the milestone began life in Lexden, was moved to Chelmsford and recut, and then returned to Lexden where it was buried in 1940. The reason for its resiting remains a mystery.

An observant drinker might notice a small milestone perched on carpeted steps in the bar at the Fox House Inn on the

122

outskirts of Sheffield (Yorks.) and would certainly wonder how it got there. The arched stone shows eight miles to Sheffield, but the inn is only seven miles from the city. The cast iron 8-mile post on the A625, the former Sheffield to Chapel en le Frith Turnpike which passes the building, is easily found a little further westward.

Churchgoers to St Botolph's in Boston (Lincs.) need to search round the side of the porch to find a milestone showing 100 miles from London against the outer wall. A suggestion has been made that it was placed there as a mounting block, and indeed the top of the stone is worn down as though it might have served this purpose. Mounting a horse from the stone's present position, however, would not have been easy, but it is hard to think of any other reason why it should have been placed there. Boston is 116 miles from London. The church archivist, a former stonemason, thinks the stone was quarried near Stamford which was closer to 100 miles from the capital on the original Great North Road. Could the milestone once have stood in Stamford, perhaps outside one of the busy coaching inns? By the early nineteenth century up to forty coaches a day passed through the town and the mileage to London would mean more to those long-distance travellers than to local people going to church or market in Boston. Perhaps the innkeeper decided to replace his milestone with a better one and sold the old stone.

Who was John Chadwick Esq. and why did he erect a milestone with a Latin inscription in 1782? It stands in Market Street, Whitworth (Lancs.) and reads 'Milliariis/primo me/-tatis et/Milliaribus/Erectis/Anno   1782/Johanne/Chadwick/de/Healey hall/Armigero/Thesaurario' (Mile distance first measured milestone erected anno 1782. John Chadwick of Healey Hall, Esquire, Bailiff). The stone must have been buried for a time because there is a record that it was found during excavations in 1911.

Recycled Milestones

Redundant milestones have found a variety of alternative and imaginative uses over the years. They were particularly valuable in areas with little or no local building material and were a useful source of ready-dressed stone. The Romans had started the trend themselves by incorporating old milestones in their own buildings. Several were found in the town wall of Clausentum (Bitterne), (Hants),[2] and one on the site of the north wall of the Roman town at Kenchester (Her. & Worcs.)[3] (see also Chapter 4: Roman Milestones). Another was found on the site of a Roman villa in Worthing (Sussex) and is dedicated to Constantine I.[4] A step in a Roman villa at Rockbourne (Hants) was found to be a milestone dedicated to Decimus (AD 249-51). It was probably never used for its original purpose because the emperor was overthrown before it could be erected.[5]

Later generations made use of what the Romans left behind. A large granite milestone from the reign of Constantine I (AD 307-37) found its way into the fourteenth-century foundations of the church in St Hilary (Cornwall), while one made of red sandstone with an inscription to the two emperors called Marcus Julius Philippus (AD 244-46) was discovered in the wall of a farmhouse near Appleby (Cumbria).[6] A cylindrical stone was found in 1910 built into a window recess of St Mary's Guild Hall in Lincoln.[7] It had marked the first mile on the Fosse Way and was dedicated to the emperor Valerian (AD 253-59). Another stone from the reign of Constantine I was unearthed in the foundations of a building in Kempsey near Worcester, and was subsequently used as part of a fence.[8]

A milestone dedicated to Aurelian (AD 173-75) was found beside the Newcastle to Carlisle road in 1932. It had been trimmed and built into a culvert.[9] A stone column seen at Willington in Co. Durham in 1794 had been squared down and used as a pillar for a cattle shed. A 5 ft (1.9 m) high rectangular slate pillar was found in 1889 as part of a stile giving access to Tintagel churchyard (Cornwall). The stone had been used for sharpening tools. Its inscription reads 'For the Emperor Caesar Galerius Valerius Licinianus Licinius' (AD 308-24).[10] An even taller Cornish milestone dedicated to Postumus (AD 258-68) was used as a gatepost at Breage near Helston, and another from the time of Gallus and Volusian (AD 251-53) had two dowel-holes cut into it to hang a gate.[11]

'The Warren/Shorne' reads a modern inscription cut on a pillar, now in Maidstone Museum (Kent). Underneath this is a Latin inscription translated as 'For our Lords Flavius Valerius Severus and Galerius Valerius Maximinus, most noble Caesars'. It dates from the period AD 305-25, and was found near the Roman road from London to Richborough, having been used in more recent times for naming a house. The Romans, however, had done their own recycling because the stone may have come from a megalithic stone circle in the vicinity. In 1836 a Roman milestone inscribed with just 'M.P.LIII' was found near Middleton (Cumbria), and was re-erected close by. The owner of the land, William Moore, carved his own Latin inscription underneath to commemorate the restoration.

Perhaps one of the most mis-used Roman milestones was that found beside the Fosse Way at Thurmaston north of Leicester in 1771 by men digging gravel. The lengthy Latin inscription, translated as 'The Emperor Caesar Trajan Hadrian Augustus, son of the deified Trajan, conqueror of Parthia, grandson of the deified Nerva, father of his country, in the fourth year of tribunician power, thrice consul, from Ratae [Leicester] 2 miles' meant nothing to the workmen, and the cylindrical stone was used as a garden roller until it attracted the attention of a scholar who realised its true significance. In 1783 the milestone, which dates from AD 120 and weighs over a ton, was incorporated into a lamp standard in Belgrave Gate, Leicester. It is now in Jewry Wall Museum, Leicester (1).

Although possibly still in their original positions, a few Roman milestones have been used as boundary markers. Their antiquity must have earned them a place in local folklore and an importance as well-known landmarks. One of these boundary stones can be found near Overtown (Lancs.) on the Roman road from Ribchester to Low Borrow Bridge. Another is near Silchester (Hants) west of the Roman town of Callena. It became known as the Impstone and was once recorded as having IMP ('For the Emperor') carved on it.

Many eighteenth-century guide stones have been re-employed in more recent years, often as gateposts. Turnpike milestones were sometimes stolen (see next section), but the turnpike trustees also sold the stones to defray the expense of having a new set made. The redundant stones have not been wasted. Robert Haynes reported in his article in *Buckinghamshire Life* that two turnpike milestones had ended up supporting a gate into the front garden of a house at Flackwell Heath (Bucks.) (see Bibliography). It is said that they were bought by a couple to be used as gravestones, although the cylindrical shape would have made them rather unusual. However, after objections to this use, they were eventually sold for £1 each and given their present function. They came originally from the Hatfield to Reading road.

A milestone that was indeed re-used as a tombstone can be found in St Paul's churchyard, Langleybury (Herts.). It marks the grave of William Rudston Faulconer who died in December 1928 aged 79. The original milestone came from the Brighton to Horsham road (Sussex) and these names can be seen carved on the back, although the mileages are no longer legible. Did Mr Faulconer have an interest in travel? The epitaph faces the busy A41 over the churchyard wall and includes a Biblical quotation - 'In journeyings often'.

When the tollhouse at Brierlow Bar (Derbys.) was demolished in the 1920s, a milestone was found to have been used as a doorstep. It showed 157 miles from London, according to A. E. and E. M. Dodd, and was repositioned nearby in the forecourt of a garage (see Bibliography). By the beginning of 1996, however, the garage was derelict and sadly the milestone was nowhere to be found. A similar piece of recycling occurred at Bell Bar (Herts.) where a milestone was used in the doorway of a cottage. In 1965 the stone was removed and set up against the cottage wall. It is dated 1745 and shows 21 miles to London. As it stands opposite the 17-mile stone in the series, it has been taken some distance from its original site. One cannot be sure that a doorstep in Bridewell Street, Wymondham (Norfolk) once stood beside the Norwich to Thetford Turnpike, but circumstantial evidence makes it seem likely. The stone has 'VIII' carved at one end, and the present milestone showing 8 miles to Norwich can be found just north of the town. This latter stone dates from the late eighteenth century, so the doorstep, if it was indeed a former milestone, probably dates from the mid-eighteenth century.

When milestones were removed in 1940 because of the fear of a German invasion, two from the Midhurst to Sheet Turnpike were taken to Petworth House (Sussex) and placed either side of the archway into the stable yard to protect it from lorries. The house was used as an army depot during World War II. The stones are still there and are in remarkably good condition. They originally stood at Rogate and Stedham and show distances to Winchester, Petersfield, Brighton, Midhurst and Petworth. The Midhurst to Sheet Turnpike was created in 1825, and these stones, over 4 ft (1.5 m) high and now clearly showing the part that would have been below ground, probably date from the early days of the Trust. One mile from the centre of Oxford on the Woodstock road, a small cylindrical milestone stands sentinel at one side of a driveway entrance. A brick pillar marks the other side of the drive. A gravestone-shaped milestone from the former Newhaven to Grindleford Turnpike (Derbys.) spent many years doing duty as a gatepost on a farm at Conksbury until it was rescued and repaired and placed at the end of a garden wall.

Old milestones have sometimes ended up as garden ornaments. A wedge-shaped stone now in Bishop Bonner's Cottages Museum, East Dereham (Norfolk) seems to have had a chequered history. It was found under a hedge a few years ago and then used as a plant stand in a lawn. From the inscription it seems to have stood originally in the nearby parish of Scarning on the road from Norwich to Swaffham. It is known from the records of the turnpike trust that the old milestones along the road, which were made in 1781, were sold when a new set of cast iron posts was ordered in 1822. Could this stone be a survivor of the original set? Another mystery is a square depression cut into the top of the stone. It is not unlike those seen in stones used to take the base of a wooden post supporting the roof of a small barn or cart shed. Near Cobham (Surrey) an old square milestone has been used to support a chain-link fence round a front garden. Although painted white like the other posts, it is conspicuous by its larger size. One of the most unusual garden features is a seat in the grounds of a Leicestershire farmhouse near Measham. Five milestones were found in a ditch on the farm, where they had probably been buried in 1940. Some of the inscriptions can still be read, giving mileages to Atherstone and Burton. The stones now form the back and sides with a wooden plank making the seat (**59**).

59 *Measham (Leics.)*

In some instances, milestones still *in situ* have been given a secondary use. Beside the A623 near Foolow (Derbys.) is a milestone that is hard to find against a dry stone wall. It has been used to support the corner of a barbed wire fence. The inscription is very worn, but the style of lettering indicates that it is eighteenth-century. One side probably read 'Tide*f*well 3/Chapel 10/Manche*f*ter 29' and the other 'Che*f*terfield/13 Miles'.

Many milestones carry the bench mark of the Ordnance Survey. The broad arrow has been an official government mark since the seventeenth century and the cross-piece, or bench, marks where the exact height above sea level has been measured from (**15,16,22,26**). The Ordnance Datum Bench Mark, or official sea level, is taken as the mean level of the sea at Newlyn, Cornwall. Bench marks are to be found on many buildings and bridges, but milestones would seem to be the least satisfactory place on which to put them as they can so easily be knocked over, dug up or buried.

Theft and Vandalism

According to a report in the *Daily Telegraph* in December 1994, thieves were removing milestones in North Yorkshire and selling them at car boot sales. However, theft and vandalism are not just twentieth-century problems. Robert Southey, in *Letters from England* published in 1807, noted that 'there is prevalent among these people a sort of mischievous manual wit, by which milestones are commonly defaced, directing posts broken, and the parapets of bridges thrown into the river'. Many of the Turnpike Acts included clauses about damage to turnpike property and the resulting punishments. The Norwich to New Buckenham Turnpike Act (1772) stated that 'if any Persons shall wilfully or designedly break, pull down, dig up, injure or destroy any of the Stones ... or erase, obliterate or deface any of the Inscriptions which shall be made thereon' they were to be fined £2 for each stone damaged. Part of the fine was to be paid to the informer and part to be used for the repair of the road. If the offenders did not pay they were to spend up to one month in 'the House of Correction or common Gaol'. Three decades earlier, the Coleshill to Chester Turnpike Act (1741) had set the fine at only £1 per stone, but if the offender had no goods and chattels to that value that could be siezed, he could be sentenced to six weeks' hard labour in prison.

It seems that these punishments did not deter vandals. A writer to *The Gentleman's Magazine* in 1778 complained that 'the milestones and direction-posts are generally mutilated and defaced by wanton and mischievous persons, to the great inconvenience and perplexity of the traveller'. He urged that 'exemplary punishments [be] inflicted upon violators'. John Farey, writing in 1817 in a book about Derbyshire, expostulated about 'those idle and disorderly persons who now so shamefully deface the milestones by their wanton and mischievous attacks on them ... scarcely a single inscription remains legible, from the peltings of the idle vagabonds ...' In 1839 the Trustees of the Norwich to Thetford Turnpike ordered the surveyor to 'use his best to find some of the old Stones which have been taken from the Road' before getting new ones made to replace them.

When 'H.C.' carved his initials on the obelisk milestone at Tixall (Staffs.) **(38)** in 1886 it is unlikely to have occurred to him that they would still be visible over one hundred years later (see Chapter 5). In 1892 'J. Thurman' left his mark on a small milestone which once stood beside the Buxton to Macclesfield Turnpike. The former coach road is now a track; the route of the turnpike was altered in 1821 to reduce the gradient. One of the roads under the jurisdiction of the New Cross Turnpike Trust ran through Bromley to Farnborough (London). The 10-mile stone in Bromley High Street suffered from the attentions of an aspiring weightlifter in 1978. The culprit was fined £25 and the stone was restored and replaced by Vauxhall College of Building. Modern pollution soon began to take its toll and it has since been given a plastic distance plate.

The ravages of the weather and of general neglect added to the mutilation by vandals. A writer to the *Taunton Courier* in 1808 protested about the illegibility of local milestones, 'in spite of the captivations of grey moss, iron staining and crumbling fragments', while in 1839 a correspondent to the *Somerset County Gazette* commented that many milestones stood 'like fools without knowledge themselves or able to impart it to others'. Assuming that an entry was made in turnpike trust minutes every time the milestones were ordered to be repainted, it would seem that this refurbishment was very erratic, and twenty years could elapse between applications of paint.

The cast iron plates on mileposts have also fallen victim to vandals and collectors. In the 1980s sandstone slabs with metal plates from Telford's series along the Buckinghamshire stretch of Watling Street were renovated or replaced. Three of the metal plates disappeared in 1986, but photographs of them existed and replicas were made. Mileposts made entirely of cast iron have been taken away for scrap, sometimes by unthinking local authorities, but also by thieves trying to make money from them. Even modern aluminium road signs are being stolen for the scrap metal value. Nowadays, however, the greatest destroyer of wayside milestones is the verge mowing machine.

CHAPTER 7

Milestones in Art, Literature and Legend

Despite being such commonplace objects in the countryside, milestones seldom appear in landscape paintings of the eighteenth and nineteenth centuries. Where they do, they are usually depicted as the typical square stone pillars of the mid-eighteenth century, examples of which can still be seen on the outskirts of London (see Chapter 4).

In J.M.W. Turner's watercolour of Prudhoe Castle, Northumberland (1825),[1] a milestone can be seen in the left foreground, clearly showing Roman numerals. In another of his paintings entitled 'Coventry, Warwickshire' (c.1830-32),[1] two stage-coaches are driving away from a turnpike gate and what looks like a milestone is located in the foreground. Turner tried to give an impression of the geography and economy of an area in his landscapes to represent the activities of the ordinary people. In 'Oxford from the Abingdon Road' (1812) a flock of sheep is being driven up the hill.[2] Something looking very like a gravestone-shaped milestone is leaning drunkenly in the grass at the edge of the road.

Constable used a square stone pillar inscribed 'Dedham Vale' to identify the location of the idyllic green valley in 'Dedham Vale: Morning' (1811).[3] Another typical square eighteenth-century milestone is shown in Hogarth's 'Chairing the Member', one of a series of prints satirising a parliamentary election in Oxfordshire in 1754.[4] The stone gives a vague mileage from London to denote whither the crowd is going with their newly elected MP.

Milestones are more likely to turn up in cartoons and coaching prints, and even those drawn in the mid-nineteenth century will often show Roman numerals, although posts using Arabic numerals had been in use for some time. In many cases the milestone is shown in the foreground with the road behind it, but if the inscription is facing the viewer, it must be on the *rear* of the milestone! Usually just a mileage is given with no specific destination. In his essay 'Dullborough Town' (*The Uncommercial Traveller*) Charles Dickens recalls a childhood memory of an oval transparency in the window of a coach office. It depicted one of the company's coaches full of happy passengers passing a milestone on the London road. With a touch of romantic nostalgia he remembers that the coach that took him away from Dullborough (Rochester) in his childhood was called Timpson's Blue-Eyed Maid, while the steam engine that brought him back many years later was merely No. 97. He was saddened to find that the coach office had been knocked down and the site was occupied by Pickfords.

Certain mass-produced picture postcards of the early twentieth century could be adapted by the printer for whichever town they were to be sold in. Some depicted a courting couple with often a signpost, but occasionally a milestone, in the scene giving the name of the relevant town. A caption at the foot of the card usually informed the recipient that the girls were miles better in this town than anywhere else **(60)**.

References to milestones can be found in literature, especially that of the great coaching era of the eighteenth and nineteenth centuries when they were the principal item of street furniture. The writers must have known the stones to which they referred, although descriptions of them are seldom given. An interesting study could be made to find if the stones in fiction are still there in fact.

Charles Dickens, in particular, was an inveterate walker, constantly seeking material for his books. 'There's milestones on the Dover road' says Mr Finching's aunt in *Little Dorrit*, and living at Gad's Hill near Rochester (Kent) Dickens would have been well aware of them. The narrator in 'The Seven Poor

Travellers' (*Christmas Stories*) imagines his travellers making their way towards Rochester on a cold Christmas Eve. 'I made them footsore; I made them weary; I made them carry packs and bundles; I made them stop by finger-posts and milestones, leaning on their bent sticks, and looking wistfully at what was written there.'

60 *Postcard c. 1909*

Milestones were much associated with weary travellers. In *Tess of the d'Urbervilles* by Thomas Hardy Tess began to grow tired as she returned from visiting her father-in-law, and she leant on gates and rested by milestones. Another of Thomas Hardy's weary travellers, Fanny Robin (*Far from the Madding Crowd*), limps slowly along the turnpike to Casterbridge (Dorchester) in the early hours of the morning. She saw the dim white shape of a milestone and drew her fingers across its face to feel the marks. Finding she had two more miles to go, she leant against the stone and rested for a short time before continuing on her way. Alison Uttley thought milestones 'the place where the tired pedestrian rested. In my imagination the characters from Hardy and Dickens stayed there' (*Country Things*).

They have found their way into local expressions, usually meaning some kind of traveller. In Cornwall a 'milestone measurer' was a tramp or highwayman, while in many other counties a 'milestone inspector' was a vagrant

134

wandering from one workhouse to another. A milestone-monger was another colloquial expression meaning a tramp. Dickens also associated them with itinerants and described an illiterate tramp pretending to read a milestone until the unsuspecting walker had drawn level and could be engaged in conversation and persuaded to part with some money ('Tramps' in *The Uncommercial Traveller*). In underworld slang a milestone was a country yokel because of the association with rural roads, while in nautical slang it was used to describe heavy seas breaking over a ship that was homeward bound because, like milestones on a country road, they seemed to make the journey slower.

Milestones were used to enhance the impression of distance travelled and, as Alison Uttley writes, they took the place of Time. Major Dobbin 'whirled rapidly from milestone to milestone, through neat country towns' in his chaise as he travelled from Southampton to London to see his beloved Amelia in Thackeray's *Vanity Fair*. In his impatience he noticed little else. Travelling at a far slower pace, Thomas Idle and Francis Goodchild set out from London one hot summer day in 1857 to walk to the north of England. As befits Dickens's *Lazy Tour of the Two Idle Apprentices*, 'the day waned and the milestones remained unconquered'. They got as far as the fifth stone from London, then decided to complete the journey by train.

They could be used in a more allegorical sense. When Joe Willett, son of the landlord of the Maypole Inn, Chigwell, in Dickens's *Barnaby Rudge*, is told that roving stones gather no moss, he replies, 'nor mile-stones much ... I'm little better than one here, and see as much of the world'. Perhaps it was no coincidence that when Joe had run away, unable to endure his father's treatment of him any longer, the landlord distributed a handbill offering a reward for his son's return, showing a boy with a bundle over his shoulder and a finger-post and milestone beside him. Perhaps the earliest traveller to be associated with a milestone was Dick Whittington, but although there really was a Richard Whittington who was Lord Mayor of London three times, he lived in the late fourteenth and early fifteenth centuries before milestones had reappeared on our roads. The Whittington Stone is situated at Highgate Hill, London.

In fact and fiction, they were useful in setting a scene and pin-pointing the exact place of the narrative. Rodney Stone in Sir Arthur Conan Doyle's eponymous story tells us that he comes from Friar's Oak, in a dip of the Downs where the forty-third milestone between London and Brighton can be seen on the outskirts of the village. The book is set at the time of the Prince Regent, and part of Conan Doyle's tale deals with a race from Brighton to London between two carriages. Although these were private vehicles, newspapers of the time contain many accounts of rival stage-coaches racing each other, often resulting in serious accidents. A fatal collision occurred at St Albans (Herts.) in August 1819 when the Chester and Holyhead Mails were racing each other down a steep hill. One man was killed and several other passengers badly injured. Following this the Post Office changed the times of the coaches so that they did not meet. The coachmen were charged with murder. The Hinckley to Leicester coach struck the post of a turnpike gate while galloping downhill to arrive ahead of a rival one day in 1815. The coachman and five of his passengers died. Much as boys of a few years ago wanted to be engine drivers, the gentry of the eighteenth and nineteenth centuries yearned to drive a stage-coach, and some fulfilled their desires. William Windham ('Mad Windham') of Felbrigg Hall (Norfolk) managed both, playing at guard, ticket-collector and occasionally engine-driver on the Eastern Counties Railway and, just before his death in 1866, driving the Norwich to Cromer stage-coach. In the mid-eighteenth century the sixth Earl of Salisbury, who lived in Hertfordshire, also amused himself by driving the public stage-coaches from London. The Marquis of Worcester and the Earl of Harborough were also on the list of aristocratic coachmen, and those who had difficulty persuading stage-coach proprietors to let them take over the reins, operated their own coach service. In Regency times, in the early nineteenth century, it was the height of fashion to be seen driving one's carriage on the

London to Brighton road. It was a good highway of ideal length and well populated with other stylish people to show off to. The Prince Regent himself boasted of driving a phaeton and four twenty-two miles in two hours at a trot. George Stubbs' painting 'The Prince of Wales's Phaeton' (1793) gives a good illustration of this type of carriage with two horses waiting to be harnessed to it.[5] This fashionable vehicle was liable to overturn, giving young men of the day a frisson of danger as they raced along the roads. The future George IV was not allowed to travel more than fifty miles from London without a government minister accompanying him. As this was very inconvenient to him it is believed that the milestones were cut to make it appear that Brighton was less than fifty miles away, when in fact it was about fifty-four. The London to Brighton road at this time started at Westminster Bridge and ran through Croydon, Redhill, Crawley, Cuckfield and Friar's Oak. It was not until 1813 that alterations to the turnpikes brought the route roughly to that followed by the modern A23. The Prince Regent was often said to have wished that he was a hundred miles from London. Perhaps it was just coincidence that Mrs Fitzherbert came from Wootton Hall near Wootton Wawen (Warwicks.) and a milestone showing this distance stands by the A3400 on the bridge over the River Alne (see Chapter 5).

In her diary for 19 May 1802, Dorothy Wordsworth wrote that she met William by the 6-mile stone before walking on to Wytheburn Water, while an anecdote from Leicestershire tells of a vicar of Melton Mowbray in the nineteenth century who rode to Leicester once a week. During his ride he sang Handel's *Messiah*, measuring his progress through the oratorio by the milestones along his route. By the time he passed the last stone he was just launching into the Hallelujah Chorus. Another story from Devon recounts that in the early nineteenth century French and American soldiers were held as prisoners of war in Ashburton. The officers were allowed some freedom and could go up to one mile from the town. Milestones were put on all the roads leading out of the town one mile from the centre, except for two stones which were a little further away to enable the prisoners, it is said, to visit a gentleman who showed them great sympathy.

Their similarity to tombstones can bring more gloomy connotations, as depicted in a poem entitled *68th Birthday* by the nineteenth-century American poet James Russell Lowell:

As life runs on, the road grows strange
With faces new, and near the end
The milestones into headstones change,
'Neath every one a friend.

In *Tess of the d'Urbervilles* Thomas Hardy describes Tess's husband, Angel Clare, and her sister, 'Liza-Lu, walking to the top of a hill overlooking Wintoncester (Winchester) to watch for the black flag to be raised over the jail to signify Tess's execution. They wait beside the first, white-painted milestone which stands on the grass verge.

Did Thomas Hardy link milestones with tombstones? Jude Fawley's ambition had long been to go to Christminster (Oxford) (*Jude the Obscure*). While lodging at Alfredston (Wantage) he walks to the summit of a hill for a view of the distant city and finds a milestone beside the road on the back of which he had carved, when he first became an apprentice stonemason, 'Thither J.F.' with a hand pointing towards the spires dimly visible on the horizon. Some years later, following many disasters in his life, he is again walking towards Christminster and stops beside the milestone. Although it is a cold, wet autumn day, he lies down to rest, hoping that exposure to the bad weather will hasten his death from tuberculosis. He feels the back of the stone and finds that his carving is still there, although almost obscured by moss. Hardy's novel was first published in 1895 as a serial in *Harper's New Monthly Magazine*. It was illustrated by William Hatherell and one scene was entitled 'Jude at the Milestone' showing a sick, lonely man clutching a blanket around him and leaning on the stone. Thomas Hardy was particularly pleased with this illustration and congratulated the artist on representing the

138

tragedy of the scene so well. Hatherell presented the author with a complete set of his illustrations for *Jude* and Hardy had them framed and hung in his study. What is now known as the 'Jude Milestone' stands at the top of Red House Hill two miles from Wantage. After being taken to the local council depot in 1940, it was not recovered until 1969 when it was erected a short distance away from its original position. It was moved back to its correct site in 1992.

Not all links with death had to be gloomy, though, as the following inscription on a tombstone in Yorkshire shows:

> This tombstone is a milestone;
> Ho, how so?
> Because beneath lies Miles,
> Who's
> Miles below.

The character of Marmaduke Milestone in Thomas Love Peacock's comic novel *Headlong Hall*, published in 1816, was a thinly disguised caricature of the landscape gardener Humphry Repton. Repton (1752-1818) had taken over the mantle of Capability Brown and worked on estates all over Britain.

One of the main forms of exercise and amusement for the landed gentry and their guests was to ride around their estates, either in carriages or on horseback. It was also quite acceptable to visit the parks of total strangers, and sometimes a carriage would be provided for the visitor on application to the head gardener. There was as much curiosity over 'stately homes' in the eighteenth century as there is today, but landowners two centuries ago were keen to show off their status symbols for their own sake and did not need to make money from them for their maintenance as is necessary today. In 1776 Mrs Philip Lybbe Powis wrote of visiting, with friends, Lord Pembroke's estate at Wilton near Salisbury. At the porter's lodge they had to write their names in a visitors' book where she noted that 2,324 people had viewed the estate the previous year.[6] The Hon. John Byng, during a journey through Oxfordshire in 1785, became quite angry when he was denied admittance to the home near Wroxton of Lord Guildford, father of the British Prime Minister Lord North, because his lordship had only just arrived from London. 'Very rude this, and unlike an old courtly lord! Let him either forbid his place entirely; open it allways; or else fix a day of admission; but, for shame, don't refuse travellers, who may have come 20 miles out of their way for a sight of the place'. An entry in *Excursions in the County of Norfolk* published in 1818 states that 'Holkham Hall is open for general inspection on Tuesdays only, except to *foreigners* and *artists*. Strangers or travellers who wish to view the house on other days can only do so by particular application to Mr Coke, who has never refused his permission.'

Repton therefore set out to create varied and interesting scenery in the park as well as impressive surroundings to the house. Although not an architect himself, he collaborated with them on the design of buildings, and was later joined by two of his sons when they had received training. After agreeing to work on an estate, he produced a book of sketches, often 'before-and-after' drawings to show how he envisaged the landscaping and its effects. These became known as his Red Books as most of them were bound in red leather, many of which have survived to this day.[7]

He wrote several books on his theories of landscape gardening, and explained how different scenes could be created, perhaps by damming a stream to form a lake, planting trees to hide a road, or taking down trees to reveal the distant view of a church. It was these ideas that sparked off the controversy over 'the picturesque' culminating in Peacock's satirical novel. Repton also thought that an indication should be given that a traveller was approaching an important house by placing a coat of arms on buildings and other objects along nearby roads. In plans drawn up in 1791 for improving Tatton in Cheshire, belonging to William Egerton MP, Repton had proposed creating a lake in the park and building a new gateway. He also suggested putting the owner's coat of arms on the market house in neighbouring Knutsford, or even on a milestone. Two former friends of Repton's, Richard Payne Knight and Uvedale Price, both wealthy, art-loving landed gentry from Herefordshire, began the quarrel in 1794 over the word *picturesque* as applied to landscape. They argued that the word could only be applied to a wild, untamed scene of boulders, gnarled trees, foaming water and perhaps a ruined building. Painters preferred a scene of 'neglect and accident' to the 'false beauty' of smooth green hills and the rounded contours of plantations created by Capability Brown and his followers.

> ... to kill or cure with strange disease
> Which gives deformity the pow'r to please;
> And shows poor Nature, shaven and defaced,
> To gratify the jaundiced eye of taste.

So wrote Payne Knight in his poem *The Landscape*. Capability Brown had died in 1783, and Repton took it upon himself to defend Brown and the art of the landscape architect from this attack by countering that a park was laid out with a view to its use and enjoyment in real life and not its appearance in a picture, and was in no less good taste.

The controversy raged for some years in poem and essay, with reviewers in the journals of the day, such as *The Gentleman's Magazine* and *Monthly Review* joining in. Horace Walpole and Edmund Burke supported the landscape gardeners, while Shelley was disgusted with all the protagonists snarling 'like an ill-trained pack of beagles'.[8]

Thomas Love Peacock satirised what he regarded as the most absurd ideas of his day. In his novel, Marmaduke Milestone arrives at Headlong Hall with a portfolio under his arm. This 'picturesque landscape gardener of the first celebrity' hopes to persuade Squire Headlong 'to put his romantic pleasure-grounds under a process of improvement, promising himself a signal triumph for his incomparable art in the difficult and, therefore, glorious achievement of polishing and trimming the rocks of Llanberris'. In a footnote, Peacock explains that

Richard Payne Knight had 'taken the liberty of laughing at a notable device of a celebrated improver, for giving greatness of character to a place, and showing an undivided extent of property, by placing the family arms on the neighbouring milestones'.

Mr Milestone observes that the land around Headlong Hall had never been touched by the finger of taste. He proposes blowing up rocks, cutting down trees, creating gravel walks, shrubberies, and canals. Some of Squire Headlong's guests disagree, objecting that it 'destroyed all the beautiful intricacies of natural luxuriance'. Marmaduke Milestone sees everything in need of 'improvement', even a pastoral scene conjured up in the words of a song. Squire Headlong eventually marries Miss Tenorina Chromatic, who sees nothing but beauty in the untrimmed woods and ivy-covered rocks, and we assume that Mr Milestone goes away disappointed.

It has so far been impossible to prove that any milestones were put up at Repton's instigation, but several are associated with estates on which he worked. At the start of his career, Repton lived at Sustead in Norfolk and became close friends with William Windham at neighbouring Felbrigg Hall. Against the wall of the stable block at Felbrigg stands a tall, gravestone-shaped milestone giving distances to Norwich, Aylsham and Cromer church, while a smaller stone stands by the lane to Sustead, its seriffed letters indicating the mileage to Felbrigg Hall and Aylsham. Although Repton lived at Harestreet in Essex from 1783 until his death in 1818, both he and his wife are buried at Aylsham. Repton also worked at Sheffield Park in Sussex in 1789 and the sandstone pillar standing at the entrance to the driveway and dating from about that time has already been described in Chapter 5. Early Ordnance Survey maps show a series of milestones along country lanes leading from Honing Hall (Norfolk) to the Norwich to North Walsham Turnpike five miles away. Two of these stones still remain. Repton worked at Honing in 1792. A privately-erected milestone stands on a country lane between Blickling and Gunton Halls in Norfolk on whose grounds Repton worked in 1794 and 1816, respectively.

It is probable that the 7th Earl of Bridgewater of Ashridge (Herts.) set up the two milestones near Pulridge on the Little Gaddesden to Hemel Hempstead road. They give distances of twenty-seven and twenty-eight miles from London. Repton worked at Ashridge in about 1811. He also drew up plans for improving the park at Longleat (Wilts.) for the Marquis of Bath in 1804. A milestone with a cast iron plate stands near Frome (Somerset) along the road from Warminster showing the distance 'Longleat/Houƒe/2 Miles'. Repton recommended that the park be left unlocked and open to visitors so that they could 'bring their refreshments' and admire the beauty of the landscape.

Although the evidence that Repton had a hand in setting up these milestones is slim, it is nonetheless an intriguing coincidence, and there may be other instances of milestones connected with the many estates on which he worked that have not yet been recorded. One estate which has milestones inside its extensive grounds, and which is unconnected with Repton is Chatsworth in Derbyshire. In the late 1830s the Duke of Devonshire had these placed on the drives to denote the mileage to the 'West Front Door including Pinetum'. The stones are sculpted in classical style, with the distance on a metal plate (**61**).

Apart from their usefulness in estimating the speed and punctuality of mail-coaches, milestones played a major role in many races. As Tom Brown goes by coach to start school in Rugby, he sees two boys waiting by the third milestone from the town. They run beside the coach to the next milestone while the guard on the coach times them (Thomas Hughes, *Tom Brown's Schooldays*). Another race, and one which can be verified, took place in Ampthill (Beds.) in 1880 when a shopkeeper, Mr White, bet that he could run faster than the local tailor's pony. The race was run between two milestones and Mr White started off well, but was soon overtaken by the pony. The exhausted shopkeeper had to be brought home in a pony and trap. Races of many kinds were staged between milestones and a large amount of money could be wagered on the outcome. While trotting horses were only required to cover distances of less than ten miles, professional 'pedestrians' would race over considerably longer distances. In 1823 a Mr Neale started from Tyburn Gate at midnight on a Monday and reached the 105th milestone on the Worcester road at 9 a.m. on the Wednesday. The following year bets were placed on Captain Parry to walk from Tyburn Gate to the 54th milestone on the Oxford road and back in twenty-four hours. Newspapers of the early nineteenth century also carried accounts of men running against stage-coaches, and occasionally of races for walking backwards.

61 *Chatsworth (Derbys.)*

It is to the child's imagination, however, that we must turn to see milestones in a more picturesque and light-hearted way. Flora Thompson's autobiographical novel *Lark Rise to Candleford* describes the childhood of Laura at the end of the nineteenth century. When the very young Laura and her brother were taken for walks along the turnpike road near the hamlet of Lark Rise (Juniper Hill) by their mother they could not pass the milestone without having the inscription read to them. They had never travelled the nineteen miles to Oxford and longed to know what the city was like. When they were old enough to go out on their own they would sometimes go to the turnpike and play leap-frog over the milestone.

Alison Uttley's description of milestones around her childhood home near Cromford (Derbys.) is written with the sharp perception of the young who could view them at a more equal level. She describes old grey stones which gave the distance to London, so linking her village with the outside world. They crouched by the walls, covered with ivy, moss and lichen. 'Many passed by without seeing them, for they were part of the road, half hidden in the green and grey clothing of the earth itself. When I walked along the road they seemed very, very far apart' (*Country Things*). 'I walked nearly three miles to school,' she says in *The Button Box*, 'and I knew the milestones very well, although they went on the main roads only. They were grey limestone triangular dwarfs, half concealed in the hedges, mossy and fern-edged, with a few violets or dry eye-bright hidden against their feet, and they had printed words and distances upon them. They only gave the names of well-known villages, and the distances were in Roman numerals. They were resting places for the weary, the tramps, the packmen, they were the meeting places for lovers, and the dens for children's play. ... We knew them personally, they were our friends, and I gave a nod of recognition to each one to tell it I remembered. The roadman kept his bag of victuals by a milestone, and many a scythe or pick was hidden by a stone ... Where are the milestones now? I miss these friends of my youth.'

CHAPTER 8

Fieldwork and Research

Local Surveys

In order to preserve milestones, it is of great help to find out as much as possible about them, and hopefully their age and local associations will excite the interest of the local authority or of concerned citizens and result in more care and attention being lavished upon them. Whether undertaking the survey of a whole county or simply finding out about a milestone in your own town or village or outside your home, it is hoped that the following notes will give an idea of how to go about seeking the information.

Many English counties now have industrial archaeology societies, and a few of these have conducted comprehensive surveys of the surviving milestones in their county. A check with a reference library in the county will ascertain whether such a study has been undertaken and a record of it published in the society's journal. Individuals have also hunted them down and compiled records, which may have been deposited with a county record office or museum. Occasionally the planning department of a county council has made a record of milestones, and it is worth enquiring there too. The Bibliography contains details of surveys which have been found by the author and which are accessible to the public. Delving deeper into the history of the milestones to find out exactly when they were made and by whom can be a time-consuming and frustrating task, but very rewarding when details are eventually found. Sometimes articles about milestones have appeared in local newspapers or county magazines, and a search of indexes in newspaper

146

libraries or a local reference library will bring them to light. If there has been no survey in your county, then it is long overdue.

Locating Milestones

The survey of Hampshire roads undertaken by the University of Southampton Industrial Archaeology Group in 1969 was a well-organised exercise involving groups of at least three people in cars - driver, observer and recorder - travelling along designated roads. Although they only covered classified roads, and also recorded such features as coaching inns, early petrol pumps, and horse troughs, about 320 milestones were sighted. At the other end of the scale, Mr D. Hamilton cycled round Suffolk recording and photographing milestones, taking his bicycle on the train to the areas furthest from his home.

There is no doubt that the best method of searching for milestones is on a bicycle with a mileometer. Cycling makes it easier to stop just where you want to, and to peer into hedges and ditches as you pass. Great care must be taken on main roads, but many stones are now on minor country lanes, and a pleasant, safe ride can be planned to hunt for them. If travelling by car, winter or spring is the best time to look, after the vegetation has died down. When one milestone in a series has been located, a check of the mileometer will give an idea when the next one is due. The distance is not always exactly a mile from the last one, and it may not be on the same side of the road. If it cannot be found immediately check carefully in hedges and ditches and poke about in long grass. It is also worth looking in nearby gardens as milestones displaced during road works have sometimes been rescued and given a home in a lawn or flower bed. A study of six inch or two-and-a-half inch (1:25,000) Ordnance Survey maps in a local reference library before your journey will give a better idea of where to look for milestones; on 1:50,000 maps they are only marked along A and B roads, and then seldom in built-up areas where there is no room to put 'MS' or 'MP'. The first or second editions of the Ordnance Survey six inch maps, produced in the late nineteenth and early twentieth centuries will give the most detailed information, and

147

often record all or part of the inscription on the stone, which is useful to know if the stone is now illegible. By locating all the stones with the same destinations, the route of an old main road can be traced, then compared with a modern map. Obelisks and monuments will often be marked on a map with no indication that they are also milestones, so these should be investigated too. Some milestones are on county registers of listed structures and county or district planning departments should have a copy of the register for their area. The entries will often give a good description and a grid reference, sometimes a very precise location and even a little historical detail.

Once found, it is useful to sketch each milestone and note its condition, what it is made of (e.g. stone, cast iron, stone with metal plate) and the style of the lettering. Measurements will also help when comparing stones in a series. Remember that milestones were made in the days of Imperial measures and they will therefore usually be an exact number of inches. Not all milestones will photograph easily, those painted black and white coming out best. Chalk can be used to pick out the lettering on unpainted stones so that it will be seen more clearly on a photograph. It will do no damage and will soon be washed off again by rain. A photographic record can be made, either of each individual stone, or of the best-preserved in each series. Many milestones have become buried in earth and vegetation and it is worth carrying a trowel with which to unearth the base. This may also reveal a date or maker's name, which was often located just above ground level when the stone was originally erected. Secateurs are sometimes useful to cut away ivy and brambles.

The information can be stored on record cards, probably best grouped by modern route numbers (A56, B1354, etc.), by a specific turnpike trust, or by place names. The front of the card could include a sketch or photograph, precise location including Ordnance Survey grid reference, full description, and the date on which the milestone was examined and its condition. The date is important because the stone may have been damaged or destroyed by the time you pass that way again. The reverse of the card can be filled with any details of the stone that emerge during the search of maps, books and documents. Use can also be made of computer databases for storing the information, making search and retrieval easier. Alternatively, notes, photographs and maps can be gathered in a loose-leaf binder to form a permanent record to be stored for future researchers. If a large survey is to be undertaken it would be worth considering making an inventory following the guidance given by the National Monuments Record Centre.[1] Their Monument Inventory Data Standard (MIDAS) was set up in 1998 to provide a common framework for recording information in order to facilitate the interchange of data with other researchers.

Locating Turnpike Routes

The first edition of the one inch Ordnance Survey maps show turnpiked roads, usually with the line on one side of the road thicker than the other. Tollgates were also usually marked. These maps have been reproduced (see Bibliography) and can be purchased in bookshops, or the originals can be consulted in reference libraries. The original route should be checked with a modern map, as the turnpike road may not now correspond with the present main road, and it may be necessary to hunt for milestones in lay-bys, by-passed villages, along country lanes which are not obviously former well-used highways or even along footpaths. Further clues to the routes of old turnpikes can be found from local names such as Turnpike Road, Tollgate Farm, Pike House Inn, and toll cottages may still exist. The word 'bar' in a place name can sometimes indicate the site of a former turnpike gate. At Hunter's Bar in Sheffield an old tollgate has been preserved in the centre of a busy roundabout, and Belchers Bar on the A447 in Leicestershire is another place name from the turnpike era. However, the name Potter's Bar seems to have originated in the fourteenth century from an entrance into Enfield Chase, and other names containing 'bar' can be derived from a gate or barrier in an ancient city wall. Names like London Road or Gloucester Road were certainly once main routes, even if they are no longer. In some parts of the country former turnpike roads were diverted or obliterated because of military activity. During World War II airfields such as Lasham (Hants) and Coltishall (Norfolk) were built across old turnpikes. Other old coaching roads, such as those across Salisbury Plain, are now out of bounds in military training areas. Milestones do still exist on roads crossing some of these army ranges, and apprentices made a new stone in 1980 to replace one that had been run over by a tank on Salisbury Plain.

Dating Milestones

Once a milestone has been located, finding archive evidence to date it is not easy, but with patience and true detective spirit it can be done. It must first be ascertained whether the stone is on a former turnpike or not. A useful list of the turnpiked roads in England is contained in *The Turnpike Road System in England 1663-1840* by William Albert (see Bibliography). The Act of Parliament setting up the Trust is also given, and the county record office or reference library may have a copy of the original Act. Some of the Acts give precise details of the route of the turnpike, although alterations and additions were often made to the route when an Act came up for renewal after twenty-one years. There may also have been articles published by the county history or industrial archaeology society on turnpike roads.

As most milestones were installed by the turnpike trusts, it is to the books of the trust that one should turn first. With luck these will be in the county records office. Sadly many are missing, but some may still exist in local solicitors' offices where they were deposited after the trust was disturnpiked. In a small town it will be possible to visit solicitors to ask if they still have any old documents, but this would be a daunting task in a large town. The search can be narrowed slightly by consulting local newspapers published during the final years of the trust (roughly the 1860s or 1870s) to look for notices of meetings of the trustees. These often give the name and address of the clerk, who was generally a solicitor, and was probably involved in winding up the trust. Local trade directories for the period may give more information about the firm, and it may then be possible to trace it through to the present day. Some district council offices or town halls may still keep documents relating to their area which may include turnpike records.

Once found, the minute books should be read carefully for any reference to milestones, and by cross-checking with the account books, if they exist, it is often possible to learn the dates, costs and makers of the stones on that particular road. More details of the craftsmen involved can be gained from local trade directories, and where there is a variety of styles of milestone on one road, perhaps some made of stone, others of cast iron, a check on the men's trades will confirm the date of manufacture. The craftsmen will usually have been 'stone and marble masons' or 'iron founders'. It may even be possible to find old business records, particularly from iron foundries, either in a county records office, a museum of local crafts and industries, or with the firm itself if it still exists. It is a good idea to check a local telephone directory; the firm's name may still be found but the nature of its business may have changed.

While reading through the turnpike minute books, it is also helpful to form a general impression of the state of the trust at different periods. Some seemed fairly affluent throughout their existence and could commission entire new sets of milestones, while others could only afford to replace those that were damaged, leaving a variety of styles which are difficult to date. If the trust was in financial difficulties when it ordered new stones, it would presumably have wanted simple ones to limit expenses.

A series of milestones on a road that was never turnpiked presents more difficulty. They may have been erected by the parish, and a search for vestry minutes or road surveyors' books in the county record office may give some information. A study of old maps can indicate the names of local landed gentry who might have had a stone put up to guide visitors to their country homes. The places named on the stone should also give a clue. The 1767 General Turnpike Act required the trusts to put the names of the main towns on their milestones, therefore any indicating a small village or a private estate suggest non-turnpike stones. Documents relating to a particular family or large estate may exist in the record office, and private correspondence may mention the placing of milestones. County and rural district councils also erected milestones from the late 1880s to the early 1900s, and it may be possible to find some information about the highway committees in the record office.

Old photographs, postcards, paintings or engravings of local scenes which include a milestone are useful clues, and a local history society, museum or reference library may have a collection, although the milestone will only be a very minor part of the picture and will probably not be mentioned in any subject index. A search of antique and collectors' shops and stalls can also be rewarding.

Some towns have a historical society which can be a very useful source of information. A library should have details of who to contact. Elderly residents may remember stones that have now disappeared, or may have seen them being buried during the war, and it might even be possible to locate and disinter them. Finding cast iron posts could be a useful task for owners of metal detectors.

Milestones on a very quiet country lane may seem puzzling, but a check of the towns or villages along the route often shows that they had regular coach or carrier services in the eighteenth or nineteenth centuries, proving that it was once a well-used road. County directories for the period should give details of such services. A search of local newspapers can often produce evidence of a coaching route in the form of advertisements or lurid accounts of accidents or crime. A paragraph that appeared in the *Norwich Mercury* in 1786 tells of a highwayman robbing a traveller on the Holt road near the 11-mile stone. This part of the road never became a turnpike, but the report shows that milestones had been set along it at quite an early date, although by what authority is not known. These routes may also have led to a large country house from the nearest turnpike road or may have been a link for local cross-country traffic between two turnpikes.

A Rough Guide to Dating Milestones

There are many exceptions to the following guidelines and therefore they cannot be taken as completely foolproof, but they will give a general idea of the probable age. If several of the features occur on one stone, the dating can be even more certain.

Roman numerals	18th century
Upright 's' (ʃ)	18th century
Old name or spelling of town	18th century
Inscription parallel to road	18th century
Made of stone	18th century onwards
Obelisk	mid-18th - early 19th century
Stone with cast iron plate	late 18th century onwards
Arabic numerals	late 18th century onwards
Inscription angled to road	late 18th century onwards
All cast iron	early 19th century onwards
County or district council	from late 1880s

Historical information about travel on English highways is widely scattered, but much can be gleaned from diaries and travel journals such as those of Celia Fiennes, John Evelyn, Daniel Defoe, Arthur Young, Parson James Woodforde, the Hon. John Byng (later Viscount Torrington), and, from the golden age of cycling, the road books of Charles Harper and the county Highways and Byways series. Novels of the eighteenth and nineteenth centuries often contain passages describing journeys which must have come from the author's personal experience (see Chapter 7).

Ideas for Further Study

Milestones come and go. They get knocked over and eventually buried in vegetation, then some years later are found again when ditches are being cleared or undergrowth cut back. Some milestone surveys were carried out in the 1960s and 1970s and it is probable that some of the stones recorded then have now disappeared and that others not found during the original survey have been rediscovered. Updating the old records and researching as much of their history as possible would be a useful exercise, if this has not been done previously. Often only small milestones from the turnpike era were included, or only those along classified roads, and larger monuments and obelisks were ignored.

It would be interesting to pinpoint more accurately the periods when the different shapes of milestones developed. To do this it would be necessary to date as many examples as possible to find the earliest year that a particular style was first used. It might then be possible to chart the development and fashion of milestone designs throughout the country. There certainly seem to be regional preferences for certain styles. Club-shaped, cast iron posts (**31**) are found almost exclusively in Derbyshire, Staffordshire and Cheshire; wedge-shaped stones (**18**) are most common in Norfolk, possibly to economise on stone in a county with no suitable local stone available; the 'circle in a rectangle' cast iron plate (**22**) is mainly confined to Dorset. Rectangular cast iron posts with pedimented tops (**34**) are found in Wiltshire, with a few in neighbouring areas of Somerset and Dorset, and may reflect a style of gravestone produced in the area. And why are rebus posts (**27**) only found in East Sussex? Did they have a particularly low literacy rate? In the latter years of the turnpike era road surveyors became more professional and were often employed by several neighbouring trusts. For ease and economy surveyors may have commissioned the same style of milestone for the roads on which they worked.

A further study could be made of the actual stone to ascertain where it came from. In counties with sources of natural building stone, there would have been little difficulty in obtaining material, and it may be possible to locate the actual quarry from which the stone was originally cut, as has already been done with Roman milestones. In areas with no such resources, however, stone would need to be brought from other parts of the country, causing greater expense. The information could give an insight into the sources of supply of local stonemasons. It is known, for instance, that several of the oldest surviving milestones in Leicestershire came from slate quarries in Charnwood Forest (see Chapter 4). Obviously, some geological knowledge is required for an in-depth survey of this kind. Some types of stone held paint better than others, and there is evidence that some of the turnpike trusts in Derbyshire sought, in particular, the product of the nearby quarries at Woodseats because of this property.

For anyone interested in the history of local firms, cast iron mileposts which show a maker's name provide evidence of the diversity of the work done by these foundries (**62**). Wootton Bros. of Coalville (Leics.) were mainly manufacturers of ironwork for the local coalmines, while the Cockey family of Frome (Somerset) started as bell founders in the early eighteenth century and by World War II were involved in the construction of gas works. Two foundries in Derby were responsible for many of the cast iron mileposts in Derbyshire: James Hayward of Phoenix Foundry (e.g. posts on the Ashbourne-Buxton road), and John Harrison of Bridge Gate (e.g. posts on the Derby-Duffield road). In Wiltshire mileposts with 'C & M W' cast at the base refer to Carson and Miller of War-minster, a firm founded in the

62 *Ardleigh (Essex)*

1820s. The large cast iron post in Tytherington is dated 1840 (**34**). Some of the Norfolk County Council posts were cast by Pertwee & Back of Great Yarmouth. The firm was founded in 1901 and manufactured a great variety of ironwork from decorative verandahs to steam engines for trawlers. It is still in business today as a car dealership. Occasionally milestones have the mason's name incised on them too.

Milestones are not just confined to roads. Canals were also provided with them, and the restoration of the waterways to cater for the increase in pleasure boating has led to the reinstatement of these milestones. They can vary just as much as those along roads, from the cast iron, V-plan posts along the Leeds-Liverpool Canal, to those looking like large, cast iron table tennis bats along the Nottingham-Beeston Canal. In 1929 several canal companies combined to form the Grand Union Canal running from London to Birmingham. Mileposts from one of these - the Grand Junction Canal Co. - can be seen near Braunston (Northants). The Lancaster Canal Society has provided modern sandstone pillars with glass fibre plates for the waterway it is restoring.

This account has been confined to 'mileage markers', i.e. those which actually state the distance to certain places, but an interesting survey could be undertaken of direction posts which give destinations but no distances. These can also come in many shapes and sizes such as the fine pillar at Fairmile (Devon) erected in memory of a missionary bishop and his two assistants who were killed in 1871 by 'savage men' in the South Seas, and, incidentally, indicating the way to such towns as Exeter and Honiton. The three-sided obelisk topped by a ball at Brampton (Cambs.) is far older and has hands pointing to London, Thrapston and Huntingdon. The 'Carved Hands' post at Wroxton (Oxon) is an elaborate square stone pillar aligned to the angle of the road (**63**). Hands carved in relief point the way to Banbury, Stratford, Chipping Norton and London. The sundial at the top faces the cardinal points and is slightly out of alignment with the lower part of the post. Another inscription explains that the post was given by Mr Francis White in 1686. Guide posts in moorland areas have been mentioned in Chapter 2. Legislation for these pre-dates that for milestones, and many guide posts are still to be found on the moors of Devon, Cornwall, Derbyshire, Yorkshire and Lancashire (**6**). A few show the mileage, but most do not. Often the spelling of the towns was quaintly phonetic and takes some interpreting. Wayside crosses can mark parish boundaries, pilgrimage routes or other tracks. Many lost the cross at the top during the Civil War and are marked on maps as 'stump cross'. Boundary markers come in many forms. In the seventeenth century the city of Oxford undertook to repair roads within one mile of the city and stones marking the limits are still in place, the one on the London road bearing the date 1667. Coventry has some smart cast iron boundary posts carrying a coat of arms and marking the city limits in 1928.[2]

63 *Wroxton (Oxon)*

Distinctive signposts, also called fingerposts, are disappearing faster than milestones, condemned by the craze for uniformity. A Ministry of Transport circular in 1921 laid down guidelines for the lettering - black block capitals three inches high on a white background - and the post also had to indicate the authority responsible for its maintenance. This still left scope for much variety; arm ends could be pointed, rounded or squared; many finials ornamenting the top were in the form of a ring displaying the county council name.[3] Other, more historic, signposts are hopefully safe. They range from those with wooden arms such as the Izod fingerpost at Cross Hands near Broadway dated 1669, Teddington Hands near Tewkesbury (both in Her. & Worcs.) and Bassett's Pole near Sutton Coldfield (Warwicks.), to a delicate wrought-iron signpost, made to celebrate Queen Victoria's diamond jubilee, which stands at Norton Lindsey (Warwicks.).

157

There are still many other turnpike remains to be seen. Tollhouses are the most obvious, and trust minute books sometimes give detailed information about their construction, even down to the dimensions of the 'necessary house' in the garden. After the disturnpiking of the roads, the tollhouses were sold and usually became private dwellings. Sadly many were demolished during more recent road widening. Their styles vary enormously from simple, rustic cottages to fine, stone buildings mimicking a more important edifice in the neighbourhood. Some were of a polygonal shape to give the tollkeeper a good view up and down the road, while the simpler dwellings may just have had a bay window or one at the side of the building to serve the same purpose. A few tollboards are still *in situ*, such as those at Butterrow, Rodborough (Glos.), Todmorden (Yorks.) and Barrowford (Lancs.). Barrowford tollhouse has been restored by the Lancashire Heritage Trust and is now let for holiday accommodation. A good number of other tollboards survive in museums. Some terminus posts are still in place; there are several good examples around Bath. A few roads still have pumps beside them which were erected at the request of the turnpike trustees. Their main purpose was to water the road to lay the dust. Many other relics of transport deserve study, for example coaching inns, cab shelters, horse troughs, and remains of the days of trams and trolley buses. Some surveys that have been done (e.g. Hampshire and Somerset) also record such items as bridges, early road signs and boundary markers.

There are even some wonderful epitaphs to be found in churchyards which relate to travel. Two examples from Norfolk will illustrate this. In the church wall at Haddiscoe, overlooking the former Yarmouth to Blythburgh Turnpike, is the epitaph to William Salter, Yarmouth stage-coachman who died in 1776. The inscription runs

Here lies Will Salter honest man
Deny it Envy if you can
True to his Business & his trust
Always punctual always just

His horses could they speak would tell
They lov'd their good old master well
His up hill work is chiefly done
His Stage is ended Race is run
One journey is remaining still
To climb up Sions holy hill
And now his faults are all forgiv'n
Elija like drive up to heaven
Take the Reward of all his Pains
And leave to other hands the Reins.

The second is a cautionary tale set above the porch of St Andrew's church, Colney which was once in good view of travellers on the Norwich to Watton Turnpike: 'Sacred To the Memory of JOHN FOX who on the 20 of Dec. 1806 in the 79th Year of his Age was unfortunately kill'd near this spot having been thrust down & trampled on by the Horses of a Waggon. Tho his Life was humble yet is it deserving of imitation He was a worthy & useful Member of Society an honest & industrious Labourer   READER   If thou drivest a team be careful & endanger not the Life of another or thine own'.   All such features can help to trace the routes of eighteenth- and nineteenth-century roads, and add to our knowledge of travel in those times.

The results of any survey should be presented to a local history society or to the county record office for the benefit of other interested people. An article could also be written for publication in the journal of the county history or industrial archaeology society, or in a county magazine, and perhaps a local newspaper could be approached with an interesting story about a local milestone, so that their plight is more widely publicised. Local authorities can be encouraged to take more interest. Derbyshire County Council has published a series of leaflets entitled 'Derbyshire Treasures'. The first leaflet, issued in 1977, was called 'Guideposts and Milestones'. A few record offices have produced teaching dossiers on the history of local roads. Many of the large milestones are now scheduled monuments, and it is the smaller ones that are most in need of protection. However, being a listed structure does not necessarily guarantee that the milestone is kept in good condition. Possibly when enough county lists have been compiled, a comprehensive record can eventually be produced of all the milestones that still exist in Britain and so help to prevent their loss.

References

References to Chapter 2

1. Now in Jewry Wall Museum, Leicester.
2. Groves, Robert: 'Roads and Tracks', in Gill, Crispin (ed.), *Dartmoor. A New Study.* Newton Abbot, 1970.
3. State Paper Domestic, 238 (1633-34), p.56.
4. Albert, William: 'Popular Opposition to Turnpike Trusts in Early Eighteenth-century England'. *Journal of Transport History*, 5, No.1 (1979) 1-17.
5. Act of Parliament 7 Geo. III c.40, para. XXX.
6. Act of Parliament 8 & 9 Will. III c.16.
7. *The History of Traffic Signs.* Dept. of Transport, 1991.

References to Chapter 3

1. Karslake, Lt-Col J.B.P.: 'Further Notes on the Old English Mile', *Geographical Journal*, 77 (1931), pp.358-60.
2. Close, Col Sir Charles: 'The Old English Mile', *Geographical Journal,* 76 (1930), pp.338-42.
3. Act of Parliament 35 Eliz. I c.6.
4. Brigg, J.J.: 'Some Old West Riding Milestones', *Yorkshire Archaeological Journal,* 22 (1912-13), pp.30-39; 23 (1914-15), pp.345-48; '"Customary" Milestones', *Yorkshire Archaeological Journal,* 30 (1930-31), pp.173-77.
5. Act of Parliament 5 Geo. IV c.74.
6. Vitruvius: *The Ten Books on Architecture*, trans. Morris Hicky Morgan. New York, 1914; repr. 1960, Ch.9.
7. Bennett, J.A. & Brown, Olivia: *The Compleat Surveyor.* Whipple Museum, Cambridge, 1982.
8. Dale, A.W.W. (ed.): *Warren's Book.* Cambridge, 1911.
9. Harley, J.B.: 'The Society of Arts and the Surveys of

English Counties 1759-1809', *Journal of the Royal Society of Arts,* 112 (1963-64), pp.43-46, 119-24, 269-75.
10.   Crone, G.R., Campbell, E.M.J. & Skelton, R.A.: 'Landmarks in British Cartography', *Geographical Journal,* 128 (1962), pp.408-30.
11.   Grant, Russell: *The Real Counties of Britain.* Oxford, 1989.

References to Chapter 4
1.   Now at Trinity College, Cambridge.
2.   Now in Buxton Museum, Derbyshire.
3.   Now in Lancaster Museum.
4.   Now in Chesters Museum, Northumberland.
5.   Now in City and County Museum, Lincoln.
6.   Now in Hereford Museum.
7.   Haverfield, F.: 'The Roman Milestone Found at Castleford', *Report of Leeds Philosophical & Literary Society,* 1897-98.
8.   Now in Carlisle Museum, Cumbria.
9.   Now in Dales Countryside Museum, Hawes, Yorkshire.
10.   *West Midlands Annual Archaeological News Sheet,* No.6 (1963) p.7.
11.   Letter reprinted in full in Phillips, Daphne: *The Great Road to Bath.* Newbury, 1983.
12.   Dale, A.W.W. (ed.): *Warren's Book.* Cambridge, 1911.
13.   Harper, C.G.: *The Cambridge, Ely and King's Lynn Road.* London, 1902.
14.   Bunce, Frank: 'The Rebus Stones of Sussex', *The Home Owner* No.105 (1961) p.21.

References to Chapter 5
1.   Webster, Norman W.: *The Great North Road.* Bath, 1974.
2.   Vaughan, Jack: 'The Stones of Shooters Hill' in *Aspects of Shooters Hill* (Shooters Hill Local History Group, 1989).

References to Chapter 6

1. Shackle, Richard: 'A Milestone at Lexden', *Colchester Archaeological Group Annual Bulletin*, Vol.33 (1990) pp.3-4.
2. Some are now in the Tudor House Museum, Southampton.
3. Now in Hereford City Museum.
4. Now in Barbican House Museum, Lewes, Sussex.
5. Now in Roman site museum, Rockbourne, Hampshire.
6. Now in Carlisle Museum, Cumbria.
7. Now in City & County Museum, Lincoln.
8. Now in Victoria Institute, Worcester.
9. Now in the Museum of Antiquities, University of Newcastle.
10. Now in south transept of Tintagel church, Cornwall.
11. Now at St Piran's, Trethevy, Cornwall.

References to Chapter 7

1. British Museum.
2. Private collection, but see Shanes, Eric: *Turner's Picturesque Views in England and Wales 1825-1838.* London, 1980.
3. Private collection, but see Parriss, Leslie: *Constable. Pictures from the Exhibition.* Tate Gallery, 1991.
4. Sir John Soane's Museum, London.
5. Her Majesty the Queen. See also Parker, Constance-Anne: *Mr Stubbs the Horse Painter.* London, 1971.
6. Simmons, Jack (ed.): *Journeys in England. An Anthology* . London, 1951.
7. Stroud, Dorothy: *Humphry Repton.* London, 1962.
8. Pevsner, N.: 'Richard Payne Knight', *Art Bulletin (USA),* 31, No.4 (1949), 293-320.

References to Chapter 8

1. Royal Commission on the Historical Monuments of England, National Monuments Record Centre, Kemble Drive, Swindon SN2 2GZ. (http://www.rchme.gov.uk/)
2. Winchester, Angus: *Discovering Parish Boundaries.* Princes Risborough, 1990.

3. Barton, Barry: 'Signs of their Times', *Cycle Touring and Campaigning* (Oct./Nov. 1996), pp.12-13.

Bibliography

Books

Aaron, Henry: *Street Furniture.* Princes Risborough, 1980.
Aaron, Henry & Sherren, Ian: *Pillar to Post. Looking at Street Furniture.* London, 1982.
Addison, Sir William: *The Old Roads of England.* London, 1980.
Albert, William: *The Turnpike Road System in England 1663-1840.* Cambridge, 1972.
Alderton, David & Booker, John: *The Batsford Guide to the Industrial Archaeology of East Anglia.* London, 1980.
Austen, Brian: *English Provincial Posts 1633-1840. A Study Based on Kent Examples.* London, 1978.
Austen, B., Cox, D. & Upton, J. (eds.): *Sussex Industrial Archaeology. A Field Guide.* Chichester, 1985.
Bagshawe, Richard W.: *Roman Roads.* Princes Risborough, 1979.
Baines, E. F.: *Forty Years at the Post-Office,* 2 vols. London, 1895.
Belloc, H.: *The Old Road.* London, 1911.
Bonser, K. J.: *The Drovers.* London, 1970.
Boumphrey, Geoffrey: *British Roads.* London, 1939.
Branigan, Keith: *Roman Britain. Life in an Imperial Province.* London, 1980.
Buchanan, Angus & Cossons, Neil: *Industrial Archaeology of the Bristol Region.* Newton Abbot, 1969.
Buchanan, R. A.: *Industrial Archaeology in Britain.* London, 1980.
Butt, John & Donnachie, Ian: *Industrial Archaeology in the British Isles.* London, 1979.
Byng, Hon. John: *The Torrington Diaries,* ed. C. Bruyn Andrews. London, 1934.
Chevallier, Raymond: *Roman Roads.* London, 1976.
Codrington, Thomas: *Roman Roads in Britain.* London, 1918.
Collingwood, R. G. & Richmond, Ian: *The Archaeology of Roman Britain.* London, rev. edn 1969.

Collingwood, R. G. & Wright, R. P.: *The Roman Inscriptions of Britain. I. Inscriptions on Stone.* Oxford, 1965.

Copeland, John: *Roads and their Traffic, 1750-1850.* Newton Abbot, 1968.

Defoe, Daniel: *A Tour through the Whole Island of Great Britain,* 2 vols. London, 1724-26.

Dodd, A. E. & Dodd, E. M.: *Peakland Roads and Trackways.* Ashbourne, 1980.

Fearn, Jacqueline: *Cast Iron.* Princes Risborough, 1990.

Hanson, Harry: *The Coaching Life.* Manchester, 1983.

Harper, Charles G.: guides to main roads in Britain such as *The Dover Road. Annals of an Ancient Turnpike.* London, 1895; *The Norwich Road: An East Anglian Highway.* London, 1901.

Haselfoot, A. J.: *The Batsford Guide to the Industrial Archaeology of South-East England.* London, 1978.

Hey, David: *Packmen, Carriers and Packhorse Roads.* Leicester, 1980.

Hindle, Brian Paul: *Roads and Trackways of the Lake District.* Ashbourne, 1984.

Hindle, Brian Paul: *Roads and Tracks and their Interpretation.* London, 1993.

Hudson, Kenneth: *Industrial Archaeology - A New Introduction.* London, 3rd edn 1976.

Hudson, Kenneth: *Street Furniture.* London, 1979.

Johnston, David E.: *An Illustrated History of Roman Roads in Britain.* Bourne End, 1979.

Majors, J. Kenneth: *Fieldwork in Industrial Archaeology.* London, 1975.

Margary, Ivan D.: *Roman Roads in Britain.* London, 1973.

Moritz, Carl Philip: *Journeys of a German in England in 1782.* London, 1965.

Morris, Christopher (ed.): *The Illustrated Journeys of Celia Fiennes 1685-c.1712.* London, 1982.

Pawson, Eric: *Transport and Economy: The Turnpike Roads of Eighteenth-century Britain.* London, 1977.

Payne, Gordon A.: *Surrey Industrial Archaeology.* London, 1977.

Raistrick, Arthur: *Industrial Archaeology. An Historical Survey.* London, 1972.

Searle, Mark: *Turnpikes and Tollbars.* 2 vols. London, c.1930.

Selway, N. C.: *The Regency Road. The Coaching Prints of James Pollard.* London, 1957.

Sherlock, R.: *Industrial Archaeology of Staffordshire.* Newton Abbot, 1976.

Simmons, Jack (ed.): *Journeys in England. An Anthology.* London, 1951.

Southey, Robert: *Letters from England.* London, 1807.

Sparkes, Ivan: *Stagecoaches and Carriages.* Bourne End, 1975.

Taylor, Christopher: *Roads and Tracks of Britain.* London, 1979.

Warren, Geoffrey: *Vanishing Street Furniture.* Newton Abbot, 1978.

Webb, Sidney & Webb, Beatrice: *English Local Government, Vol.5: The Story of the King's Highway.* London, 1913.

Willcocks, R. M.: *England's Postal History to 1840.* Perth, 1975.

Woodforde, James: *The Diary of a Country Parson 1758-1802.* Oxford, 1978.

Wright, Geoffrey N.: *Roads and Trackways of the Yorkshire Dales.* Ashbourne, 1985.

Wright, Geoffrey N.: *Roads and Trackways in Wessex.* Ashbourne, 1988.

Wright, Geoffrey, N.: *Turnpike Roads.* Princes Risborough, 1992.

Milestones are sometimes mentioned in other field guides to industrial archaeology published by the Association for Industrial Archaeology (AIA), Batsford, and David & Charles. Reproductions of first edition one inch to one mile Ordnance Survey maps originally published between 1805 and 1873 are produced by David & Charles of Newton Abbot.

Articles

The following articles and booklets cover substantial surveys in a particular area or good general information on milestones. Many small articles exist in local newspapers and magazines, and regional reference libraries should be consulted for these. If any articles have been omitted, I apologise and can only blame the difficulty of tracking them down.

Austen, Brian & Upton, John: 'East Sussex Milestones - A Survey', *Sussex Industrial History,* no.5 (Winter 1972/73), pp.2-13.

Austen, Brian & Upton, John: 'East Sussex Milestones - Further Notes', *Sussex Industrial History,* no.7 (Spring 1976), pp.23-24.

Bentley, J.B. & Murless, B.J.: *Somerset Roads. The Legacy of the Turnpikes.* Somerset Industrial Archaeology Society, *Phase 1 - Western Somerset* (1985); *Phase 2 - Eastern Somerset* (1987).

Branch Johnson, W.: 'Hertfordshire Milestones', *Journal of Industrial Archaeology,* 2 (1965), pp.184-85.

Brown, Bernard: '"As the Crow Flies". Milestones in Metropolitan Kent', *Bygone Kent,* 9, no.3 (1988), pp.179-84.

Cossons, Neil: 'Turnpike Roads of the Bristol Region - A Preliminary Study', *Bristol Industrial Archaeology Society,* 1 (1968), pp.6-13.

Cox, Benjamin G.: *The Vale of Evesham Turnpikes, Tollgates and Milestones.* Vale of Evesham Historical Society, 1980.

Cox, Christopher: 'Milestones of the Stroud District', *Transactions of the Bristol & Gloucester Archaeological Society,* 33 (1964), pp.119-42.

Cox, Christopher: 'Some Problems of Dating Milestones', *Industrial Archaeology,* 6, No.1 (1969), pp.60-69.

Cox, Christopher & Surry, Nigel: 'The Archaeology of Turnpike Roads', *Journal of Industrial Archaeology,* 2 (1965), pp.33-40.

French, E.C.W.: 'Turnpike Trusts', *The Amateur Historian* 2, No.1 (1954), pp.4-7.

Gow, W. G.: *Dorset Milestone Survey* (Dorchester, 1980).

Haines, Carol: 'Norfolk Milestones', *Journal of the Norfolk Industrial Archaeology Society,* 4, No.1 (1986), pp.27-30; 4, No.2 (1987), pp.46-52; 4, No.4 (1989), pp.137-42; 5, No.1 (1991), pp.34-42; 5, No.3 (1993), pp.193-99; 5, No.5 (1995), pp.363-72; 6, No.2 (1997), pp.35-45.

Hart, R. J.: 'A Survey of the Milestones in Western Berkshire', *Berkshire Archaeological Journal,* 67 (1973/74), pp.71-77.

Haynes, R.I.E.: 'Buckinghamshire Milestones'. *Buckinghamshire Life* (November 1966), pp.17-19.

Haynes, R.I.E.: 'Wiltshire Milestones', *County Councils Gazette* (June 1968).

Hosier, F. Audrey: 'The Measured Mile', *Old Cornwall,* 9, No.11 (Autumn 1984), pp.544-56; 9, No.12 (Spring 1985), pp.576-86; 10, No.1 (Autumn 1985), pp.2-9; 10, No.2 (Spring 1986), pp.55-62; 10, No.3 (Autumn 1986), pp.105-12.

Lawrence, Keith: 'Milestones of Oxfordshire', Oxfordshire Museums Service, Information Sheet 7, c.1977.

Morley, Don: 'Nottinghamshire Milestones', *Nottinghamshire Industrial Archaeology,* 8, pt.2 (March 1983), pp.1-13.

Rees, S. Allan: 'Turnpike Roads of the Bristol Area Survey - Part 2', *Bristol Industrial Archaeology Society,* 5 (1972), pp.19-24.

Rosevear, Alan: 'Milestones and Toll-houses on Old Turnpike Roads', from Rosevear, Alan: *Roads Across the Upper Thames Valley,* 1994.

Viner, D. J.: 'The Industrial Archaeology of Hampshire Roads: A Survey', *Hampshire Field Club & Archaeological Society Proceedings,* 26 (1969), pp.155-72.

Other Surveys of Milestones

Some survey records available to the public include:

Berkshire (eastern): H. W. Copsey (Reading Museum).

Hampshire: Southampton University Industrial Archaeology Group (Special Collections, University of Southampton Library).

Hertfordshire: W. Branch Johnson (Hertfordshire Record Office, Hertford).

Suffolk: D. A. Hamilton (Suffolk Record Office, Bury St Edmunds).

Gazetteer

The following list records most of the milestones mentioned in this book by county, place, Ordnance Survey grid reference, and the relevant page in the book giving further information. Entries in bold refer to an illustration number and not a page number. Entries with an s under the grid reference denote a series of two or more milestones of the same pattern along a road; those with an m signify that the milestone is in a museum.

COUNTY/Place	OS Grid Ref.	Page No
BEDFORDSHIRE		
Ampthill	SP 034381	67,104,**45**
Potton	TL 223491	67
BERKSHIRE		
Chilton-Arlington	s	69
Knowl Hill	SU 820791	45,71
Maidenhead-Twyford	s	71
Newbury-Marlborough (Wilts.)	s	71
BUCKINGHAMSHIRE		
Amersham-Tatling End	s	66
Aston Sandford	SP 762066	66
Aylesbury-Tring (Herts.)	s	84
Brackley-Buckingham	s	74
Chalfont St Peter	TQ 002924	97
Dashwood's Hill	SU 794949	66
Fenny Stratford	SP 885339	81
Haddenham	SP 757107	85
High Wycombe-Stokenchurch	s	66
Longwick	SP 778061	67
Longwick	SP 789048	67
Marlow	SU 849867	97
Warrington	SP 896531	85

| West Wycombe | SU 833946 | 100,**41** |
| Winslow | SP 766283 | 118 |

CAMBRIDGESHIRE (inc.Huntingdonshire)
Alconbury	TL 186783	99
Balsham	TL 585508	113
Barton	TL 403550	89
Bassingbourn	TL 348434	66
Cambridge (Castle Str.)	TL 444592	109
Cambridge (Hill Rd/Station Rd)	TL 457573	65
Cambridge-Barkway (Herts.)	s	62, **15**
Caxton	TL 302587	66
Chatteris	TL 383833	90,**35**
Fowlmere	TL 417442	63,**15**
Godmanchester	TL 260703	86
Melbourn (A505/B1368)	TL 408430	64
St Ives	TL 322722	95
St Ives-Potton (Beds.)	s	67
Trumpington	TL 452569	63

CHESHIRE
Audlem	SJ 654431	29
Bradley Mount	SJ 911774	75
Cat & Fiddle Inn	SK 999723	130
Chester	SJ 395633	29
Chester (Northgate Str.)	SJ 404665	108
Knutsford-Macclesfield	s	89
Macclesfield-Buxton (Derbys.)	s	88
Waverton	SJ 458617	29,86,**7**

CORNWALL
Bearland	SX 348699	39
Callington	SX 355689	40
Callington-Liskeard (A390)	s	120
Callington-Saltash (A388)	s	120
Callington-Tavistock (Devon) (A390)	s	120

Crows-an-Wra	SW 402275	72
Hendrabridge	SX 264654	42
Liskeard (Lostwithiel rd)	SX 248646	42
Liskeard (Torpoint rd)	SX 260640	42
Little Comfort	SX 346808	119
Trerulefoot	SX 328589	39
Zennor	SW 438374	117

CUMBRIA

Ambleside	NY 385020	111
Brampton	NY 519594	78
Brigsteer	SD 484894	90,**33**
Cartmel	SD 379786	111,**49**
Cartmel	SD 388801	117
Dent	SD 697873	121
Frostrow	SD 686914	23
Kendal	SD 515924	16
Kirkby Thore	NY 620264	57
Leagate	NY 540005	89
Middleton	SD 623858	57,125
Rydal	NY 366060	111
Tebay	SD 629978	38

DERBYSHIRE

Alfreton	SK 409558	118
Allestree	SK 350399	88,155
Ashbourne	SK 175469	65
Ashbourne-Buxton	s	155
Ashbourne-Haddon	s	70,72,**18**
Ashbourne-Leek (Staffs.)	s	88,154,**31**
Ashford in the Water	SK 197697	88
Baslow	SK 250718	88
Buxton-Macclesfield (Cheshire)	s	88
Chapel-en-le-Frith-Sheffield (Yorks)	s	84
Chatsworth	SK 262706	143,**61**
Conksbury	SK 210654	127
Darley Dale	SK 275628	112

Derby-Duffield	s	88,155
Foolow	SK 195761	128
Grindleford	SK 246779	113
Swadlincote	SK 292216	112
Thorpe	SK 150497	74

DEVON

Ashcombe	SX 903792	40
Copplestone	SS 776024	119,**55**
Exeter-Barnstaple	s	119,**55**
Lipton Hill	SX 491553	120
Moretonhampstead	SX 755857	40,120,**11**
Okehampton-Tavistock	s	120
Tavistock-Callington (Cornwall)(A390)	s	120
Torquay	SX 908672	112
Torquay	SX 911644	120,**56**

DORSET

Bradford Abbas	ST 590141	108
Charminster-Buckland Newton	s	77,154,**22**
Dorchester (High West Street)	SY 690907	46,110
Dorchester (Maiden Newton rd)	SY 673928	77
Dorchester-Sherborne	s	69
Edmondsham	ST 048124	87
Lulworth	SY 802803	113
Minterne Magna	ST 658045	69
Shaftesbury-Salisbury (Wilts.)	s	69
Shaftesbury-Warminster (Wilts.)	s	67
Sherborne	ST 638181	90
Sherborne	ST 627175	90
Sherborne-Yetminster	s	77
Stinsford	SY 709913	57
West Stour	ST 762218	87
Winfrith Newburgh	SY 835864	77

173

DURHAM, Co.

Darlington	m	44
Darlington (Allan Str.)	NZ 299153	44
Easington	NZ 412430	121

ESSEX

Ardleigh	TM 057297	84,**62**
Coggeshall	TM 853222	114,**51**
Earls Colne	TM 860289	87
Gt Bentley	TM 101235	86,**30**
Harwich	TM 252308	114
Lexden	TL 967251	122

GLOUCESTERSHIRE (inc. Bristol)

Bath-Tetbury	s	76
Bulls Cross	SO 877087	104
Cainscross	SO 835049	107
Cam	SO 749036	119
Chipping Camden	SP 151391	114,**52**
Chipping Sodbury	ST 730821	46
Kingsdown	ST 818672	77
Marshfield	ST 783739	43
Nailsworth	ST 848999	119
Nympsfield	SO 797003	119
Painswick	SO 864088	119
Southmead	ST 572777	74

HAMPSHIRE

Andover-Newbury (Berks.)	s	72
Andover-Salisbury (Wilts.)	s	79
Chandler's Ford	SU 429193	75
Christchurch-Fordingbridge	s	87
Corhampton-Bishop's Waltham	s	74
Farringdon	SU 704352	76
Fordingbridge	SU 151140	118
Lymington-Christchurch	s	120
Lyndhurst-Christchurch	s	79,120
Shalden	SU 708437	75

| Silchester | SU 609624 | 125 |
| Southampton | SU 418147 | 75,120,**21** |

HEREFORD & WORCESTER
Bacton	SO 380325	29
Beckford	SO 974357	102,**44**
Bredon	SO 919368	97
Broadway	SP 089381	103
Hardwicke	SO 276437	87
Ross-on-Wye-Welsh border (A40)	s	87
Worcester-Bromyard (A44)	s	31

HERTFORDSHIRE
Barkway	TL 385536	64
Barkway-Cambridge (Cambs.)	s	63
Bell Bar	TL 252054	126
Hatfield-St Albans	s	86
Langleybury	TL 080006	126
Puckeridge	TL 377243	47
Puckeridge-Barkway	s	75
Pulridge	TL 002119	143
Pulridge	TL 011109	143
St Albans (Luton rd)	TL 148100	84
St Albans (Watling Street)	TL 127088	81
St Albans (Watling Street)	TL 137078	81
Stevenage-Biggleswade	s	66
Tonwell	TL 329181	17
Tring-Aylesbury (Bucks.)	s	84
Wadesmill-Royston	s	75

KENT
Bexley	TQ 507728	45,110
Broughton Aluph	TR 033467	74
Canterbury	TR 147580	15,45,**3**
Flimwell-Rye (Sussex)	s	76
Southborough	TQ 580444	75
Westerham-Ashdown Forest (Sussex)	s	92

175

LANCASHIRE

Bacup	SD 869244	112
Barnacre	SD 495441	72,**20**
Cabus	SD 491462	43
Dunsop Bridge	SD 657499	38
Forton	SD 490524	77,**23**
Helmshore	SD 782206	40
Lancaster-Clitheroe	s	122
Longridge	SD 702414	38
Overtown	SD 630761	125
Preston-Garstang (A6/B6430)	s	72,**20**
Trough of Bowland	SD 622530	107
Whitworth	SD 883183	123
Wilpshire	SD 696332	72

LEICESTERSHIRE (inc. Rutland)

Ashby-de-la-Zouch	SK 360168	69
Breedon-on-the-Hill	SK 402228	86
Ibstock	SK 415100	69
Leicester (Belgrave Gate)	m	68
Leicester (Hinckley rd)	m	74
Leicester (Mkt Harboro-Desboro rd)	m	69
Leicester-Uppingham	s	69
Leicester-Welford	s	91
Loughborough-Burton	s	86
Lutterworth (A426)	SP 544842	91,112,**36**
Lutterworth (A427)	SP 539845	91
Measham	SK 347124	128,**59**
Morcott (A47)	SK 925003	86
Morcott (A6121)	SK 925003	86
Walcote	SP 571838	91

LINCOLNSHIRE

Bicker Bar	TF 237382	30
Boston	TF 326441	123
Holbeach	TF 359248	110,**48**
Long Sutton	TF 420237	72

Normanton	SK 949463	105
Sutton Bridge	TF 478212	85
LONDON, Greater		
Barnes Common	TQ 230759	45,66,**13**
Barnet	TQ 247979	105
Beckenham	TQ 374695	45,62,**10**
Bromley	TQ 402690	130
Clapham (A3)	s	46
Ealing	TQ 185805	85
East Sheen	TQ 203753	46,65
Eltham (Avery Hill)	TQ 438745	45
Eltham (Foot's Cray Rd)	TQ 434737	45
Hampstead	TQ 264857	28
Haverstock Hill	TQ 279846	44
Highgate	TQ 282872	27
Kensington	TQ 257796	85
Knightsbridge	TQ 263795	45,91
Richmond	TQ 177745	47,95
Roehampton	TQ 220755	65
Shooter's Hill	TQ 432765	106
Snaresbrook	TQ 399881	46,98
Southwark	TQ 314792	40,46,94, **37**
Sutton	TQ 258645	66
MANCHESTER, Greater		
Urmston	SJ 755949	107
MERSEYSIDE		
Rainhill	SJ 491914	113
NORFOLK		
Acle	TG 401105	107
Attleborough	TM 049953	106,**46**
Billingford	TG 008202	30
Blickling	TG 165285	65,**16**
Blickling (Gunton rd)	TG 186288	142
Bramerton	TG 292050	43
Burgh St Margaret	TG 449139	30,155

177

Crimplesham	TF 648046	30
East Dereham	m	127
Felbrigg Hall	TG 193394	142
Filby	TG 464135	30,155
Fransham	TF 912125	77
Fransham	TF 897117	77
Gorleston	TG 526050	43,84,**29**
Gt Yarmouth-N.Walsham	s	30
Haddiscoe	TM 445968	107
Holt Obelisk	TG 077387	99
Holt	TG 086391	40
Honing	TG 326280	142
Honing	TG 328288	142
Ingoldisthorpe	TF 683328	122,**58**
Mattishall	TG 051111	118
North Elmham	TF 987214	74,112,**50**
Norwich-Cromer	s	30
Norwich-Fakenham	s	117
Norwich-Watton	s	70
Outwell	TF 532028	90
Poringland	TG 267023	104
Raveningham	TM 392964	101
Sustead	TG 207366	142
Welney	TL 524950	120
Wymondham	TG 111013	127

NORTHAMPTONSHIRE

Daventry	SP 566629	81
Desborough	SP 802832	101
Oundle	TL 036881	109,**47**
Thrapston	TL 003790	43
Towcester	SP 694484	118,**54**

NORTHUMBERLAND

Alnwick	NU 190147	121
Alnwick-Belford	s	86,121,**57**
Alnwick-N.Sunderland	s	89
Birtley	NY 912816	57
Chesterholm	NY 772664	57
Colwell	NY 948747	68,121,**17**

Denwick	NU 180145	89,**32**
Hedgeley	NU 054187	89
Henshaw	NY 757663	57
Little Swinburn	NY 960769	68,117,**53**
Morpeth-Alnwick (Old A1)	s	121
Otterburn	NY 877935	70
Rothbury-Hexham	s	67,121,**17**

NOTTINGHAMSHIRE
Gamston	SK 687766	102
Markham Moor	SK 718740	102,**42**
Nottingham	SK 532384	69
Oldcotes	SK 588878	30
Ranby	SK 655808	118
Southwell	SK 701539	108
Worksop (Mansfield rd)	SK 565784	78
Worksop (A60)	SK 587818	120

OXFORDSHIRE
Badbury	SU 265945	67
Dorchester-on-Thames-Henley	s	71
Headington	SP 534065	67
Headington (Bury Knowle Park)	SP 648072	71
Oxford (Woodstock rd)	SP 506087	127
Oxford (Abingdon rd)	SP 519040	78
Thame	SP 707061	109
Wantage	SU 394849	139

SHROPSHIRE
Bromfield	SO 480769	43
Craven Arms	SO 433827	98
Ironbridge	SJ 669035	112,118
Ironbridge (Blists Hill)	m	39,81,**26**
Norbury	SO 365923	117
Oswestry	SJ 299309	81
Shrewsbury	SJ 467133	81

SOMERSET (inc. Bath)

Coxley	ST 527434	87
Dinnington	ST 395122	78
Frome (Bath rd)	ST 780485	43
Frome (Warminster rd)	ST 791446	143
Greinton	ST 407361	92
Ilminster	ST 347151	78,**24**
Kilmersdon-Norton St Philip	s	87
Long Cross	ST 654454	77
Nettlebridge	ST 648486	87
North Brewham	ST 742372	74
Shepton Mallet	ST 601439	30
Shepton Mallet (market cross)	ST 618436	112,155
Stoke-sub-Hamdon	ST 463168	78
Stratton-on-the-Fosse	ST 666525	42
Wells	ST 538446	90
West Camel	ST 578253	74
Wincanton-Hindon (Wilts.)	s	74
Wincanton-Ilchester	s	74
Yarlington	ST 664289	77

STAFFORDSHIRE

Alstonefield	SK 127560	86
Burton upon Trent	SK 257232	43
Burton-Abbots Bromley	s	86
Leek-Ashbourne (Derbys.)	s	88,154,**31**
Morridge Side	SK 019541	88,154,**31**
Shugborough	m	92
Tixall	SJ 975226	96,130, **38**

SUFFOLK

Bramfield	TM 399741	84
Hadleigh	TM 026425	97,**39**
Nayland	TL 975343	97
Newmarket	TL 655647	84
Woodbridge	TM 274491	112

SURREY

Burntcommon	TQ 038547	45
Cobham	TQ 118616	128
Cranleigh	TQ 061390	105
Esher (Claremont Park)	TQ 134630	45,46,66
Esher (White Lady)	TQ 147655	45,99,**40**
Godstone	TQ 350521	46,66
Lingfield-Hailsham (Sussex)	s	82

SUSSEX

Ashdown Forest-Westerham (Kent)	s	92
Hailsham-Lingfield (Surrey)	s	82
Isfield	TQ 450156	47,82,154, **27**
Lewes	TQ 411100	45,46,109, 118
Petworth	SU 976220	127
Rye-Flimwell (Kent)	s	76
Sheffield Park	TQ 411246	45,100,118 142
Uckfield-Lewes	s	47,82,**27**
Wych Cross (wall)	TQ 419317	110
Wych Cross (rebus)	TQ 419325	83,**28**

WARWICKSHIRE

Atherstone	SP 304971	77
Dunchurch (obelisk)	SP 485712	96
Dunchurch (mounting block)	SP 475715	104
Harbury	SP 393595	43,**12**
Henley in Arden	SP 151656	108
Lower Shuckburgh	SP 493624	84
Newbold on Stour	SP 245467	100
Upper Brailes	SP 304400	79,**25**
Wootton Wawen	SP 155631	113,137

WILTSHIRE

Alderbury	SU 210247	68
Amesbury	SU 140417	67
Beckhampton	SU 007692	71,**19**
Box	ST 842688	45
Chitterne-Yarnbury Castle	s	67
Hindon-Wincanton (Somerset)	s	74
Marlborough-Cherhill	s	71
Marlborough-Newbury (Berks.)	s	71
Mere	ST 830345	67
Salisbury-Andover (Hants)	s	79
Salisbury-Shaftesbury (Dorset)	s	69
Tytherington	ST 914410	43,90,154, 155,**34**
Warminster area	s	90
Warminster-Shaftesbury (Dorset)	s	67

YORKSHIRE

Ackworth	SE 441172	102
Ackworth	SE 440177	102,**43**
Anderby Steeple	SE 333921	91
Birdwell	SE 346007	96
Bramham	SE 418443	23
Bramhope	SE 241440	43
Grangemoor	SE 221154	23,83,**5**
Hebden Bridge	SD 958275	72
Ingleton	SD 792815	23
Long Preston	SD 829585	23
Malton-York	s	92
Otterington	SE 359911	86
Pateley Bridge	SE 160653	118
Richmond	NZ 146009	30
Richmond (Green Bridge)	NZ 169005	113
Rotherham	SK 435915	43
Sedbusk (Mile House Farm)	SD 883908	31,92,122

Sedbusk	SD 898905	122
Sheffield (Fox House Inn)	SK 266802	122
Skipton	SE 017528	23
Slack	SD 977287	72
Stone Chair	SE 118279	104
Swinithwaite	SE 045892	30,92,**8**
Thirsk	SE 432821	27
Todmorden (Reddyshore Scout Gate)	SD 941202	38
Todmorden (Salter Rake)	SD 944230	38

Index

local authorities 29-31, 53, 81, 82, 92, 107, 122, 131, 139, 146, 148, 151, 152, 157, 159
London 8, 14, 16, 18, 27, 37, 44-47, 53, 104, 135, 136
London Stone 10, 42
Lowell, James Russell 138
Luxembourg, milestones in 10

Macadam, John Loudon 22, 79
mail-coaches (see: coaches)
Manchester 13, 18
maps 48-54
Metcalfe, John 22
mile
    customary 37-38, 104
    measurements 35
    statute 36-37, 49
milestones (see also: monuments; obelisks, Roman)
    benefactors 17, 24, 62, 65, 99, 103
    cast iron 83-92
    geology 59, 61, 65, 68, 75, 80, 154
    metal plates 73-79
    multi-purpose 103-107
    re-used 56, 58, 123-29
    stone 60-72
    walls 45, 93, 107-12
monuments 45, 93, 99-103, 148, 154
Moritz, Carl-Philip 1, 95
mounting blocks 93, 103-104, 123

Norfolk 4, 15, 17, 18, 24, 27, 42, 136, 140, 142, 150, 152, 154, 155, 158
    turnpike trusts 15, 22, 30, 70, 76, 90, 107, 117, 118, 127, 129 130, 158, 159
Northamptonshire 14, 143, 156
    turnpike trusts 84
Northumberland 18, 52, 57, 59, 132
    turnpike trusts 70
Nottinghamshire 4, 102
    turnpike trusts 78

obelisks 46, 47, 67, 94-98, 99, 104, 105, 130, 148, 156
Ogilby, John 37, 41, 46, 49-50
Ordnance Survey 4, 50, 52-53, 128, 142, 147, 149
Oxfordshire 52, 132, 139, 144, 156
    turnpike trusts 71

packhorse roads 13, 24-26, 33,
Peacock, Thomas Love 139, 141-42
pilgrim roads 11, 157
place names
    abbreviated 39, 86, 87, 89, 118-22
    historic 61, 67, 68, 69, 74, 75, 87, 100, 109, 118-20, 153
pole 36, 39, 40, 41

vandalism (see: crime)

Wales 20, 27, 56, 79, 81
Walpole, Horace 14, 141
Warren, Dr William 41, 42,
    62-65
Warwickshire 4, 27, 132,
    137, 157
    turnpike trusts 43, 84
Watkins, Alfred 8, 40
Whittington Stone 136
Wiltshire 4, 14, 74, 139, 143,
    150, 154, 155
    turnpike trusts 68, 71
Wordsworth, William 111,
    137
World War II 3, 11, 32, 38,
    67, 69, 73, 81, 83, 91,
    106, 112, 122, 127, 128,
    139, 150, 152, 155

Yorkshire 18, 20, 22, 25, 26,
    27, 30, 36, 38, 58, 59,
    129, 139, 149, 156, 158
    turnpike trusts 22, 23, 31,
    123
Young, Arthur 14, 79, 153

zero milestone 118

NOTES

NOTES

NOTES

NOTES